A Successful Woman's Handbook:

Fifty-one Ways to Build your Community of Clients Online

How Women are Using the Web to Grow their Business, Reach the Right Customers, and Make a Difference

Monica S. Flores

A Successful Woman's Handbook:
Fifty-one Ways to Build your Community of Clients Online

Copyright © 2008 by Monica S. Flores.
Artwork © Genesis A. Lodise.
Cover photograph used with permission.

All rights reserved. No part of this publication book may be reproduced, stored in a retrieval system or transmitted in any form or by any means, electronic, mechanical, photocopying, recording or otherwise without the written permission of the publisher.

For more information:
http://www.asuccessfulwoman.com

ISBN: 1-4348-1627-3
ISBN-13: 978-1-4348-1627-6

Printed in the United States of America
July 2008

Dedication

This book is dedicated to the women worldwide who are giving their all and striving to create a better world through their ideas. Thanks to all of you for sharing your talents, skills, and your aspirations through your businesses.

I also dedicate this handbook, with love and appreciation, to my grandparents, Rodolfo, Clara, Mauricio, and Victoria.

-M. S. F.

Preface

Because of my work, I meet a number of stellar individuals. These include: professional women who inspire me to greater heights of achievement, organizational directors who challenge me to be more effective, and simple heroes who give me hope and inspiration for our shared world. I've enjoyed meeting many positive women and people who build up communities, and I've compiled this first book in the "Successful Woman" handbook series to encourage you to find ways to apply your own energy to your chosen field of work in a practical, meaningful, and helpful way.

The purpose of this book is to share with you my insights from the web development field and to show you ways to energize and activate your website. I predict that when you implement these tips, your whole business, including solutions you provide on your website, will increase in leads, connections, and sales.

In the fifty-one tips in this book, I give you specific action items to increase the vitality of your website. As you implement these tips, you'll add a big boost to your bottom line. Follow the instructions, use the checklists, and measure your results as you go through each tip.

I hope this book will give you insight into how to translate your natural enthusiasm, skills, and gifts into your web presence. When your website functions as a go-to destination for people and when people immediately think of your website as a great source for information, you truly become part of the web of interconnectedness that touches us all.

As your business or organization grows, you will reach more and more people. As you help others, you will have the chance to provide tremendous value to your customers, and you also have the chance to foster connectedness, empowerment, and generosity in your own community.

In my last decade of work, I've witnessed abundant, overflowing opportunities for women in business. Whether you are new in business or you're an established pro, I encourage you to seek out other women and support them. When we all work together, we all rise together.

I encourage you to "put yourself out there" with your positive energy and your ideas to create value, enjoyment, and fulfillment for others. Start out with a side job or strike out on your own. With the right support, tools, and a rocking website, you'll grow your business and use your profits to benefit your loved ones and the causes that you support. I am honored to support you in this process.

Monica S. Flores
July 18, 2008

Contents

Chapter 1: Website Basics   1

Your Website as an Extension of Your Company   2
Tip 1
    Prepare Yourself: How Much Does It Cost?   4
Tip 2
    Think About your Content: Explain it Well   9
Tip 3
    Design Necessities: Be Bold and Succinct   13
Tip 4
    Your "About Us" Page: Encourage Trust   16
Tip 5
    Think About the User: Be Respectful   18
Tip 6
    Best Practices for Multimedia   20
Tip 7
    Provide New Features based on Feedback   22
Tip 8
    Maintain your Site Update your Pages   24
Tip 9
    Lay Down the Ground Rules: Terms of Use   27
Tip 10
    Keep Contact Information Current   29
Tip 11
    Change is Not Always Good   31
Tip 12
    Make it Simple, Keep it Real   33
Summary to Keep in Mind: Website Basics   35

Chapter 2: Share Your Knowledge　37

Why Share? Reasons Why Giving is Good　38
Tip 13
　Blog it: Be an Authority in your Field　40
Tip 14
　Calendar It: Display Relevant Industry Events　49
Tip 15
　White Papers: Create an Online Brain Trust　51
Tip 16
　Interactive Items: Add Calculators and Estimators for Sticky Effect　53
Tip 17
　Dig Deep: Provide "Ask the Expert" Pages　55
Tip 18
　Make it Fun: Add a Quiz or Poll　57
Tip 19
　Control Junk E-Mail: Create an Opt-in List　59
Tip 20
　You're Linked In: Be an Answer Provider　62
Tip 21
　Forums: Provide Answers for your Community　64
Tip 22
　Placement: Add a Link to your Signature　66
Tip 23
　Lighten Up: Humor Makes Visitors Happy　68
Tip 24
　Be a Good Guest Host: Network and Share　70
Summary to Keep in Mind: Share your Knowledge　72

Chapter 3: Build a Resource List　75

Be a Resource to your Customers　76

Tip 25
    You're a Clearinghouse: Link to Subject Matter   79
Tip 26
    Show your Trust: Provide Referral Links   81
Tip 27
    Share Links: High Quality means High Results   86
Summary to Keep in Mind: Build a Resource List   88

Chapter 4: Target your Clients   91

Finding the Right People Means Focusing   92
Tip 28
    Be Personable: Meet People Online and Offline   94
Tip 29
    Use Social Networking: An Overview   99
Tip 30
    Show, Don't Tell: Add a Demonstration   111
Tip 31
    Comment Thoughtfully on Other Sites   114
Tip 32
    Are you Legitimate? Add Testimonials   116
Tip 33
    Photo Gallery: Provide Samples of your Work   120
Tip 34
    Share your Values: Report on your Vision   123
Summary to Keep in Mind: Target your Clients   125

Chapter 5: Focus on Usability   129

If They Can't Use It, They Won't Use It   130
Tip 35
    Browser Basics: Elements of your Layout   132

Tip 36
    The Queen of Links: Check for Error Pages   *134*
Tip 37
    Standards: Move to a CSS Version   *136*
Tip 38
    The Extras: Audio, Video, and Flash   *138*
Tip 39
    Share How it Works: Add a Checklist   *140*
Tip 40
    Help Your Visitors: Use Easy Navigation   *142*
Tip 41
    Whip Out the Credit Card: Encourage Online Payments   *144*
Tip 42
    A Call to Action: Offer it on Every Page   *146*
Summary to Keep in Mind: Focus on Usability   *147*

Chapter 6: Measuring Data   151

How to Inform Your Decisions   *152*
Tip 43
    The Welcome Mat: Understand Who's Dropping By   *153*
Tip 44
    Build the Path: Improve User "Flow"   *157*
Tip 45
    Keep 'em Coming: Make your site "Sticky"   *159*
Tip 46
    Data Tells the Truth: Use Your Site Reports   *161*
Tip 47
    For Community-building: Expanding your Reach   *163*

Summary to Keep in Mind: Measure Your Data   168

Chapter 7: Final Tips   171

Final Thoughts on Making Your Website Work   172
Tip 48
    Search Engines: Use Keywords Effectively   174
Tip 49
    Site maps and Robots and Spiders, Oh My!   176
Tip 50
    Serving Your Clients: the Ultimate Goal   178
Tip 51
    Knowledge = Results: Publish in Print, too   180
Summary to Keep in Mind: Tidy up the Loose Ends   182

Chapter 8: Extra Special Touches   185

Finishing Touches   186
One-Minute Primer on HTML   187
Check for Errors on Forms   190
Spam Catchers: Protect Yourself   191
No Phishing: Protect Your Identity   192
Images, Tables and Alternative Text   194
Fostering Security   195
Summary to Keep in Mind: Website Evolution is Natural   198

Conclusion   201

Resource List   203

Acknowledgments

My heartfelt appreciation and thanks go to the following people who helped make this book a reality:

My husband and son, who gave me flexibility, time, and all their support. I am so grateful for your presence in my daily life.

Rob Seidenspinner, of Sage Circle Coaching, counselor *extraordinaire*, for challenging me to connect with my inner self, speak my truth, and live authentically.

Special thanks to all the entrepreneurs and business owners with whom I've had the pleasure of meeting over the last few years. Your dedication truly inspires me.

Many thanks to my Mom and Dad, to Carmen and Dan, Sylvia and Garrett, and to my extended family: Yonie, Carmelo, Sara, Pat, Liz, Sally and Myrna.

Special acknowledgments and a big hug of appreciation and gratitude go to Helen Harris, who read my very first drafts and made useful suggestions. I also thank Stephanie Spann for her expert assistance as my editor and to Sandy Diaz for her valuable advice. Thanks to Christine Flores for additional editing and to Genesis Lodise for incorporating the changes.

Special thanks are due to this book's earliest supporters: Sally Durgan, Johanna Silva, Becky-Joe ChongTim, Shauna Handrahan, Cynthia Borcena, Kevin Maes, Jayeesha Dutta, Neil Kripalani, Laurie Silverman, Madhavi Jagdish, Corin Ramos, Johanna Silva, Reena Flores, Stephanie Lu, Susan Gunelius, Jeannine Schumm, Bob Valderrama, Alice Lai-Bitker, Susanna Ordway, Joanne Fedeyko, Mary Valderrama, Ann Jordan, Corey Gibb, Catherine Davenport, Christina Flores, and Nancy Brown. You all give me so much support and encouragement.

Thank you!

Introduction

Many of us who are deep in the world of web design and development are constantly innovating, trying out new tools, creating new solutions, and surfing online for the latest and greatest. We tend to forget, however, that the typical businessperson is also deep in her own world of inventory, product line development, marketing, sales, cash flow, and staff management. The ultimate answer for all of us is to create systems that reduce the need for us to actually be there and to find efficient ways to give all of us more money, time, and freedom. If you're in business for yourself or you're working to support a company or client you care about, I am happy to share some of the tips and tools I've learned "in the trenches" over my last ten years of creating websites.

Why should you listen? In 1999, I hand-coded one of my earliest websites in exchange for internet access at a café near Lago de Atitlán, Guatemala. I used my rickety old laptop and took photos on my trusty SONY Mavica (a camera that takes pictures directly onto a floppy disk). The proprietors were thrilled with the results, which allowed them to market to the then-burgeoning market of English-speaking travelers checking e-mail. They put their site up on free Tripod hosting, and they were up and running within a day, publicizing their link through flyers and word-of-mouth. It was a win for them, a win for me, and this transformational experience hooked me on translating web technology into tangible financial results for clients.

Since that first website, I've directly coded thousands of web pages for clients who rely on their websites for positive cash flow. I've also envisioned and implemented different solutions to help our clients manage their processes and directly increase their bottom line. Technology is always changing, but along with other web resource people listed in the back of this book, I am in business to fully utilize the democratizing power of the Internet. We've learned much of what works and what doesn't work, and we're happy to share this information with you.

For my own business, 100% of my new clients come from referrals and the contact form posted on my company's website. Between our web presence and our toll-free access line, we've created ways that allow our partners to work wherever we have access to an internet connection. I think in today's globalized society we will expect that an influential blogger may be based in New Zealand, or that a retailer may be updating her product line from her home in Quito or Capetown, or that a fashion marketer may be working remotely from Winnipeg. Tools like Earth Class Mail (digital delivery for snail mail), Ring Central (toll free numbers and voice mail forwarding), virtual assistants, and digital wireless help people work from anywhere around the world. Our astronauts already send photos from the International Space Station, so within the next few decades, I fully expect bloggers to upload their videos from a lunar base!

This book lays out the basics of what you need to successfully use your website as a profitable business solution. I've compiled and numbered the fifty-one tips and organized them into themes that comprise separate chapters. I encourage you to review each tip and incorporate the action items into your existing website, if you have one. If you don't yet have a web presence, use the book to plan out your content and then connect with a web professional from the resource guide in the back. I feel comfortable recommending each of these web workers listed in the guide.

Chapter 1: Website Basics. Understand the basics of healthy web functioning and you'll learn the specific units that constitute your website.

Chapter 2: Share Your Knowledge. Discover ways to become a resource provider in your specific field.

Chapter 3: Build a Resource List. Learn how to assemble and display valuable resources on your site and make it a comprehensive "go-to" destination for information about your industry.

Chapter 4: Target Your Clients. Find ways to discern, "hook," and capture your most valuable and targeted customers. You'd rather have one highly desirable and desired client than one hundred non-interested prospectives. Use the listed tips to find your best customers.

Chapter 5: Focus on Usability. Familiarize yourself with various ways to ensure your website displays well for all your visitors. I emphasize relying less on external services and more on good keyword and tagging practices, optimized text, and tools that allow search engines to understand and crawl your website.

Chapter 6: Measuring Data. An introduction to specific metrics to track and understand your website results. With data and reporting, you get a continuous sense of how visitors use your website. Use these tips to increase your conversion rate and turn your tentative strangers into beloved customers and friends.

Chapter 7: Final Tips. Additional expert tips to make the most of your website functioning.

Chapter 8: Extra Special Touches. A bonus section with a number of extra "finishing" ideas to polish your website and make it shine.

The ***Conclusion*** wraps everything up, and the back section offers a ***Resource List*** of active, smart, helpful web professionals.

I've crafted the fifty-one tips with the goal of identifying and "catching" key moments when a typical business website evolves: from being a static brochure site, to becoming a dynamic database-driven site, to providing original content and tools, to functioning as a valued resource, to securing you the status of trusted advisor to your larger community.

I end each chapter with a section to "Keep in Mind" that revisits the main "take home" messages.

Before we begin, I invite you to take a moment to ask yourself several important questions about your current website.
- Is it working for you?
- Is it sending you qualified leads?
- Are clients and customers finding you through your website?
- Are you using the website to process requests and to provide tools and downloads?
- Do new customers understand your business and use the website to get started with becoming a client with you?
- Do existing customers find all the FAQs and tools they need on your site?

Whether you own a multimillion dollar company and are looking for techniques to improve business or you are a first timer about to launch a new enterprise, implement the following tips, and check your results every month to watch for improvement. I invite you to visit me online at my own site: www.ASuccessfulWoman.com, where there are valuable up-to-date resources, information, and tools to support you.

Your business is a unique expression of the values and vision you have for your company. The products and services, brand, marketing and sales approach, and, indeed, your whole life is connected to the holistic spirit of your company. Make your unique viewpoint work for you. All of your ideas flow directly from you into your external materials, so identify and embrace the special qualities that set you and your business apart from others.

I trust you'll find innovative ways to make your website function as a valued and valuable part of your business process. Use your website to process forms, provide quotes, do minor calculations, and collect basic paperwork. These powerful tools will make your own job (or the jobs of your employees) easier.

There is only one of you in the world, and the World Wide Web gives you wonderful chances to share your ideas. I look forward to supporting you in your success.

YOUR WEBSITE DETAILS:

1) Domain Name/s: (www.yourlink.com)

2) Hosting Details:

    Provider:

    Customer Number:

    FTP login and password information:

Control Panel login and password information:

    Other passwords:

Chapter 1: Website Basics

- Your Website as an Extension of your Company
- 1. Prepare Yourself: How Much does it Cost?
- 2. Think about your Content: Explain it Well
- 3. Design Necessities: Be Bold and Succinct
- 4. Your "About Us" Page: Encourage Trust
- 5. Think About the User: Be Respectful
- 6. Best Practices for Multimedia
- 7. Provide New Features based on Feedback
- 8. Maintain your Site: Update your Pages
- 9. Lay Down the Ground Rules: Terms of Use
- 10. Keep Contact Information Current
- 11. Change is Not Always Good
- 12. Make it Simple, Keep it Real
- Summary to Keep in Mind: Website Basics

Your Website as an Extension of Your Company

Our global information age means that your website is not optional. It is expected. Our 24/7 mentality also means that your website will be queried during and outside of your personal working hours. When you clearly label information, you do more than make it easy for a visitor to find an answer to her question, understand your pricing, or sign up for an account with your business. You also establish an automatic advantage because your website works for you, both as an integral part of your business process and as a means of extending your company's accessibility and reach.

As you add website functionality and your site becomes more user-friendly and easier to understand, you'll contact an increasing number of customers; and as you grow your customer base, you'll automate even more procedures on your website. I recommend that you constantly brainstorm ways to increase your website efficiency to provide value to your business and to your customers. Work with a trusted web advisor to enhance functioning, boost your company's reputation, and improve your business processes.

Monitor your website statistics to get a good sense of who is visiting you, how visitors interact with your site, and which search terms they use to find you. Use feedback directly from your users to increase your website functionality and make more sales online.

Describe your Ideal Website Flow, which is your best vision for how you want the website to work for your company. For my company, this starts with a visitor being referred by an affiliate or former client to my website. Next, the visitor reviews my portfolio, learns more about my available products, and views testimonials on who else has implemented these same products. My web visitor uses an online estimator to review which of my proposed solutions fits her organization's budget. Finally, she contacts us through my website contact form: the client explains her situation and sends me her initial information and order. In this business model, my next step is to fulfill the order according to the company's posted guidelines.

Your ideal situation may include some additional steps, like filling out required forms or booking an appointment online, but the basic premise is that your website helps you make more sales and helps process any required information.

Tip 1
Prepare Yourself: How Much Does It Cost?

Your website is the most efficient way to utilize advertising dollars. It is always open, can target potential customers, explain your offerings, demonstrate your process, and offer valuable information. Most people prefer to sit at home in pajamas and surf the Internet instead of calling you directly. Give these web visitors an opportunity to learn more about your company through an effectively designed interface.

There are many design options available, all of which serve to establish your reputation, encourage trust, and provide an easy way for your customer to say "Yes." Whatever you offer, your website is an engaging and interactive medium. It is as important and possibly "stickier" than print, radio, and television.

When you convert your visitors into customers, the real magic begins! An expert web developer will assist you in making this process a smooth one. While estimating the costs of your website, you should keep four items in mind: domains, hosting, files, and maintenance.

All websites are made of a domain (the www.yourname.com link), a hosting package (where the files "live"), and the actual files of your website. Maintenance or ongoing updates to your files are an additional, negotiable cost. The domain is a fixed cost of between $8 - $25/year (as of 2008), with most business owners retaining control of the .COM, .ORG, and .NET versions of their names. Hosting is a fixed cost, between $50 - $200 per year, with most providers offering standard options like a control panel and open source tools like PHP and mySQL databases. You can also maintain your own server to host your own files.

A web designer/developer typically comes up with a quote to design and develop your website files, which include pages, images, and multimedia. Additional items such as search engine optimization, e-mail setup, and web marketing may be extra line items in your quoted estimate.

After you sign off on a design, your web resource person "unpacks" the built files onto your hosting package. A good web developer will give you a range of options (from open source Content

Management Systems to blog platforms to proprietary tools) that fit your budget and your needs.

Maintenance trends change constantly. You've probably heard of clients who are "locked in" to a potentially draining ongoing relationship with their existing web designer (who often charges $20, $40, $70, or $100 per hour for monthly maintenance). The industry is moving away from this codependent relationship and more towards the separation of form and content, with greater reliance on automated tools.

A typical scenario now looks like this:
1) You receive web designs (from $50 to $450 per design)
2) Your web team encodes your site (budget between $55 to $150/page depending on page complexity)
3) You access content management tools for your site
4) You build internal capacity to make future data changes in-house or with a data entry staff person

If you are comfortable using web-based forms, convert to a database-driven system as soon as possible. You may then move your web maintenance or product inventory management in-house. Then you can focus on using your web team for highly functional updates that support your business, like installing mailing lists, adding plugins, developing new forms, creating members-only content with logins and passwords, deploying payment systems, or installing an e-commerce solution.

At 10K Webdesign, one of our company mottos is "fire your web designer." You'll want to work yourself out of any position where you're dependent on a web developer who "holds your website hostage." Believe me, your web developer does not want to do data entry maintenance: she realizes that you understand your business best; and if she's good, she'll want to get back to her main business of building new sites and improving existing ones. Your web developer will give you tools to get your job done, as easily and as simply as possible.

As your website grows in complexity, you'll want to move increasing web functionality and web maintenance needs in-house, and you will work with your web developer in ways that maximize the value of her expert input.

Typically, a web developer focuses on building new sites and increasing functionality on your existing site by adding new forms or expanding interactive elements. A web designer focuses on creating new templates or new designs for your homepage or secondary pages. A web content manager focuses on data entry and creating new content on the site.

Checklist of website pieces for your quote:
- [ ] Domain name
- [ ] Hosting
- [ ] Design/Graphics
- [ ] Multimedia elements
- [ ] Content management system
- [ ] Maintenance
- [ ] Additional content updates
- [ ] E-mail
- [ ] Website statistics
- [ ] Website reporting
- [ ] Plan for making upgrades
- [ ] Staff roles and responsibilities
- [ ] What is your responsibility as the client?
- [ ] Technical assumptions, if any
- [ ] Main contact

Tip 2
Think About your Content: Explain it Well

In your website, as in your business, the quality of your content is queen.
- Who do you attract to your business?
- What key words or phrases does your target audience use?
- Which qualities set your business apart from your competitors?
- How does your company help customers?
- Why is your business unique?

I encourage you to consider your website content carefully and organize it around five main sections: Home, About, Products and Services, Testimonials, and a Contact Page. Additional pages assist your customer in making the decision to trust you.

When a web visitor comes to your site, having found you through a referred link or a search engine query, you have less than ten seconds to capture her attention.

"Who are you? What are you about? Do you have what I want? Who else uses your products or services? How do I contact you?" These are the questions your visitor has, so answer them!

Content on the web is very different from print content. You don't need "filler" text, which is difficult for the eye to read on a computer or mobile screen.

Here are some guidelines to developing your content:

A) **Use answers to these basic questions to structure the information on your website:**
Who are you?
What do you do?
Where are you located?
When are you available to help me?
How do you help?
Why should I choose you?
How do I contact you?
What's the next step to doing business with you?

B) **Avoid excess verbiage:** Edit your text, cut out "white noise" and make strategic use of keywords and phrases to connect with your target customers.

C) **Use bullet points and lists:** Lists are much easier for visitors to process.

D) **Show, don't tell:** Use samples as often as possible. A graphic designer shows slides of her work. A bath and body products store displays pictures of its products. An architect shows pictures of finished buildings. A musician plays samples of her music.

E) **Use active verbs:** "We fix BMWs" is much more effective than "If you have an automotive maintenance need, we have the capacity to help."

As you receive feedback from your employees and customers, you'll refine your content so people seeking you may find you with a minimum of cognitive effort. Make it easy for your visitors by being absolutely clear.

Checklist for your content:
- [ ] Keywords identified and added to pages
- [ ] Clearly labeled content and navigation
- [ ] Navigation is easy to understand
- [ ] Active voice

- ☐ "About Us" includes pictures of staff or partners
- ☐ Offerings and prices clearly listed
- ☐ Policies listed out (shipping, returns, privacy, legal)
- ☐ Contact information on every page
- ☐ Images and videos, if necessary
- ☐ Each page spell-checked and edited for clarity
- ☐ Content "matches" or improves upon your existing marketing communications text
- ☐ Printer-friendly pages, if needed
- ☐ Downloads, if any, available in PDF format
- ☐ Cryptic notation kept to a minimum
- ☐ Icons, if used, are easy to understand
- ☐ Broken links repaired
- ☐ General "look-and-feel" conveys professionalism
- ☐ Use the website to answer frequently asked questions from your buyers

Tip 3
Design Necessities:
Be Bold and Succinct

The look and feel of your site conveys important clues to your users about your industry, your company's standards, and your organization's quality. Certain designs trigger certain reactions and expectations in your visitors. Pay particular attention to color, layout, font style, and user interface.

As you go through the web design process, consider your message and your target client. Other websites in your field may yield clues, so do a search for your competitors or partners. Sometimes stereotypes do play a role. Sites targeting women are typically pink or other pastel colors and have rounded shapes and edges, while sites targeting men are deeper colors with more angular edges. Add pictures of people if yours is a service-related business. Never go with a design that you don't like; your site represents you and your company, so make sure your design fits your overall brand.

Color is a major indicator of the overall function of a site. There is a reason why most financial sites are white and blue; similarly, food-related sites are shades of green, brown, and red, and gaming sites are in black or dark green with white script. Choose an overall palette and stick with it.

At my web development company, we always recommend that you use sans-serif fonts for your text, and we recommend that you minimize the types of fonts and the variations in font-size that display on any web page. Use color, bolds, or italics to specify different headings and sub-headings.

When you implement your layout, provide obvious signposts and visual clues to your visitor. When navigation is consistent, your user feels comfortable clicking because she is confident of where she is and where she is going. Develop a "flow" so the typical user goes from her normal questions to eminently clear answers. When a business website is clearly laid out, the user stays. When a business website is clearly laid out and includes engaging content, the user stays longer, visits more pages, and typically becomes more deeply involved.

Typically, visitors move from the homepage, to the "About Us" page, to your packages and prices, then to the testimonials and gallery page. If they like what they see, they continue to your contact or signup page. Create your pages with customers' needs in mind so you can help your user.

As I said earlier, when a website is clearly laid out, the user stays. When it is "sticky," meaning highly informative and engaging, the user stays longer. Generate "stickiness" by adding resource materials such as white papers, blog entries, articles, checklists, behind-the-scenes videos, images, stories, and "top 10" lists. By extending your ability to capture visitors, you provide more opportunities for a potential customer to feel comfortable with your expertise. Keep resource materials in a special box or in a highlighted section, and add your contact information, a form, or an e-mail sign-up box to continue the user's experience with your business.

Checklist for what to include on your website:
☐ Color appropriate to your industry?
☐ Clear layout?
☐ Sans-serif fonts (recommended)?
☐ Pathways: next steps clearly laid out for your visitors?
☐ Test your site on associates: do they find what they're looking for? Is your site easy to use?

Tip 4
Your "About Us" Page: Encourage Trust

Humans naturally want to know with whom they're dealing. Are you a robot spammer or are you a live person? Prove it in your "About Us" page, which displays information and pictures about the company's directors, partners, and staff. In today's information overload society people have so much anonymous interaction that they appreciate any effort to personalize business interactions.

I encourage you to add photos of your key players to your "About Us" page. These help make your company real to your visitors. If you're a real person, you will have a real picture, a statement, a mini-biography (three paragraphs maximum), and a contact link. Add personal information to the extent that it enhances your credentials or provides insight into your character. People naturally like to know your interests, so if your hobbies or activities are appropriate and personable, feel free to include them.

Potential investors, partners, and clients will appreciate that you are a real person who puts your name and your image on display as a representative of your company.

Your "About Us" page connects naturally with the "Contact" page. List out the correct person to contact for a specific function (e.g. "Grace Lee is our VP of business development", or "for wholesale inquiries, please contact Anita Roberts").

Checklist for what to include in your "about" page:
- [ ] Picture of key player (Are you real?)
- [ ] Name and Title listed (Who are you?)
- [ ] Brief biography or statement (What do you do?)
- [ ] Personalized (Why should your customer care?)
- [ ] Phone number, e-mail, or link to contact form

Tip 5
Think About the User: Be Respectful

Before going live with any of your website content, consider if the content is respectful, informative, and engaging enough to deserve display space. Also make sure your text is properly formatted, spell-checked, and grammatically correct. Crop and optimize images so they reduce the impact of load times for your page.

Since your users have just a few minutes to make up their minds about your service, give them adequate information to help them come to a favorable decision. When you make unsubstantiated claims or outlandish promises that no one is able to deliver or when you use any kind of "pushy" or even abusive language, your users will feel irritated, and your site will become off-putting. If you provide ground rules and a checklist of how you work or if you state your values and your mission and provide helpful related information, your users will feel that you're on their side.

Being respectful of your visitors' time means sharing, but not shouting. It means understanding their needs and proposing strategic solutions. It means giving them enough information to make an informed decision. Respect will propel you a long way forward in business: use it or lose it.

Checklist for a web visitor's ease of use:
- [ ] Formatted text?
- [ ] Spell-checked content?
- [ ] Punctuation used well?
- [ ] Rework excessively promotional language?
- [ ] Provide resources/evidence to help with decision-making?
- [ ] Call to action on every page?
- [ ] Are you respectful? Are you sure?

Tip 6
Best Practices for Multimedia

When web designers first started using graphical buttons, most of us thought they were a good idea. However, we found that if typical website visitors didn't recognize a graphical button as a clickable button, they never thought to use it. In short, the graphical element didn't "register" for them.

By now, most people understand clickable buttons, but not everyone's machine has the latest upgrade for multimedia. For example, when you rely very heavily on Flash, music, or images to explain your message, make sure that your typical website users understand what you are using. If they lack the right software, your user won't even realize that something is missing.

When you check your website on your own machine, you may see and hear a clickable dollar bill with a video of an engaging spokesperson, but one of your potential users may see an error message or a broken link, or she may hear a voice and not know its origin.

Make sure that all of your visitors understand what's happening on your website. You may want to add links to the latest software versions so users can download and append these plugins to their browser.

When you use Flash, audio, or video as navigational elements or if you rely heavily on graphically-intensive elements in your content, make sure that your site offers alternate versions and alternate text for users without the latest plugin. However, if you have a multimedia gallery, a gaming site, or an entertainment-related site, these guidelines may be relaxed, as most of your web users have the appropriate tools to view your pages.

Tip 7
Provide New Features based on Feedback

As you start to receive feedback or requests through your website, you will probably begin to hear the same comments or similar questions from multiple visitors. In response to these types of feedback, consider implementing new features that match your users' needs as they emerge.

Examples of inexpensive new features include a FAQs page, a quote generator, and automatic sign-up systems. Your "Frequently-Asked Questions" section gives a confused visitor a good place to start. A quote or estimate calculator gives visitors an opportunity to make rough estimates online. Automatic membership and login sections give your users immediate access to the parts of your website they require.

Additional features that may be helpful include forums or bulletin boards with questions and answers from other community members, automatic payment systems to direct users to an electronic download, or a "forms" page with required PDFs.

As your business grows, you will automate even more basic procedures so the "flow" your web visitors experience approximates the intake procedure an on-site client receives.

Checklist for business processes online:
☐ Which paper forms may you convert to web-based forms?
☐ Which functions do your customers constantly ask for?
☐ May parts of your customer service be automated on the web?
☐ Do you offer online payments?
☐ Can a customer change an address online, or do holds or cancellations online?
☐ Forgotten passwords may be resent?
☐ Forms may be downloaded in PDF format?
☐ Registrations or applications available online?

Tip 8
Maintain your Site
Update your Pages

As search engines visit your site, they check to see the "time stamp" on your page. When a site is updated on a regular basis (at least every four months for static pages, with more dynamic pages updated weekly or monthly), the search engine assumes that the page is "relevant," and the search directory adds those links to the current set of results. When your content on your website has become outdated, the search engine (rightly) assumes that the page is no longer relevant. You may see your page ranking drop at this point.

Some excellent ways to add additional pages to your website include using blog software, displaying event calendar updates, using an image updater to add more timely content to your site, or highlighting announcements.

Blog entries provide "fodder" for search engines. When they are tagged and specific to your field of expertise and when they include a link back to your homepage, you have an instant "link bait" system that provides additional ways for potential customers to find you. For example, my blog publicizes other women in business, refers visitors to book reviews, provides opinions and news, and also directs clients to my web design company. I receive direct feedback and tips from readers, which encourages me to provide even more timely information on the blog, which in turn brings more potential clients to my company. It's a continuous cycle that benefits both my blog and my business.

"Feeds" export data from your applications and "push the data" to another location. An example of this would be publicizing your latest blog posts in a sidebar of your corporate website. Other kinds of "feeds" include adding randomized images from your constantly uploaded stack of online photos, putting an event calendar with upcoming events on your site, providing a news feed with press releases from your company, or publicizing your latest newsletters, clients, or resource papers.

When you incorporate these routines into your standard business practice, you'll have at your disposal ways to implement timely "messaging" as part of your regular company procedures. With these tools, you can, for example, publish a monthly "roundup" of new events, papers, clients, or industry news: and then you can use this roundup to create an updated blog entry and a news page for your website.

Checklist for ways to keep your pages fresh:
- [ ] Blog posts
- [ ] Photo gallery or visitor photo gallery
- [ ] Event calendar or visitor event calendar
- [ ] Latest press releases
- [ ] Latest newsletter
- [ ] Recent projects or upcoming projects
- [ ] RFP list
- [ ] Job opportunities or volunteer opportunities
- [ ] News archive
- [ ] White papers
- [ ] Published articles
- [ ] Member highlights
- [ ] Customer highlights
- [ ] Story of the month
- [ ] Notes from our director
- [ ] Seasonal announcement
- [ ] Staff profile
- [ ] Latest volunteer projects or newest volunteers
- [ ] Industry news
- [ ] Company announcements
- [ ] Recent awards
- [ ] Who's who
- [ ] Expert analysis
- [ ] Charitable giving report

Tip 9
Lay Down the Ground Rules: Terms of Use

If your e-mail box is free of junk mail, congratulations. You're one of the few people whose e-mail addresses didn't "escape" into the wild world of Internet bulk mailers. If you do receive unwanted e-mail, you know how important it is to offer privacy and confidentiality to your own clients who entrust you with their e-mail and contact information. Offer the following pages in a clear posted place: your privacy policy, your terms and conditions of use, and your policies regarding data sharing. We encourage you to display links to these items from every page, typically on a sidebar or on the bottom of the page in the footer area.

Add a link to your privacy policy from any contact form or order form where you require customer information. Also add a link to your privacy policy whenever you offer a "Send This Page to a Friend" function. Add a terms and conditions of use page to inform visitors about how to use your site and to protect you from copyright infringement. Add your shipping, payment, and return policies for more transparency and for ease of customer accessibility.

There are a number of other ways you may demonstrate your company's thoughtfulness about website usage. Consider featuring a "Logos" page where you offer different sizes of your logo to those who want to link to your pages or who need print quality versions of your logo. Offer head shots in various sizes for your company staff. Additionally, if you're willing to allow links to your website from other websites, make this clear by offering a "link policy" page with instructions on how to appropriately link to your website.

If you have a counter that keeps track of the number of web visitors your site has received, keep it in a low-profile place as sometimes this graphic may be too overwhelming. You may want to include a copyright notice with your legal company name, your number of years in business, and how to contact you. You may have a Better Business Bureau certification or other directory certifications such as "Fair Trade Certified" or "Green Business." You may also be a part of a membership organization. Place these small graphics in your footer, and link to your directory listing or to a page that describes the importance of that membership.

Tip 10
Keep Contact Information Current

While I don't encourage you to put your cell phone number on the sidebar of your blog (like well-known technology guru Robert Scoble does), I do encourage you to put a clear link to your contact information at the bottom or on the side of every page. Your customers, associates, and friends want to contact you, so give them clear instructions on how to do so.

Since people like to connect with you by phone, via e-mail, or in person, I suggest covering all three preferred methods: put your phone number on every page, include a link to your e-mail contact form, and post a list of any events, seminars, or panels that you're attending or your company is sponsoring.

An e-mail contact form on your website does not need to show your actual e-mail address. One tip is to convert the e-mail link into a graphic (to reduce spam) or hide it in language only a real, live human may decode, like this: monica (at) asuccessfulwoman (dot) com. Alternatively, have your web developer "hide" the e-mail address within the form that processes and sends the e-mail message.

If you have multiple staff members, use a succinct explanation to direct your visitors to the right person to get their questions answered. For example, "for media and press inquiries, please visit our "Press Releases" page, or contact Jane Garcia at jane.garcia@yourwebsite.com". Some simple instructions will reduce confusion on your visitor's part.

You may want to sign up for a "Recaptcha.net" account, which offers your developer a snippet of code to further protect your e-mail address or website contact form submissions. This "captcha" deters automatic spammer programs and encourages a live person to read and type in two separate words to prove they are a real website user and not a machine.

Tip 11
Change is Not Always Good

If you haven't visited Craigslist.org, you might want to take a look at this immensely successful community bulletin board service, which is organized around geographical locations and subject areas. The site is clean and easy to understand; it has black text with blue links on a white background, and it hasn't changed since its inception. The enduring quality of Craigslist.org is part of its appeal: you always know what to expect when you visit. The content may change, but the format does not.

Change, when it comes, may be disconcerting to your regular visitors. If you already have a certain look-and-feel for your site and you want to change it around a little bit, consider retaining some of the major elements, such as your logo, tag line, and color palette. If you do make a major change to your website design, navigation, logos, or functionality, your regular visitors may be taken aback or, even worse, may not know if they are on the correct site.

PayPal, Amazon, and Yahoo! have undergone design changes over the years, but the overall feel and functionality of these sites remain consistent over time. For your website, it's expected that you'll constantly make updates. However, if you're making major changes to the style of your site, find ways to retain the flavor and spirit of your original website over successive iterations. Announce any website changes in a prominent place like your news section or alert box. Also, make sure any outdated links redirect to the correct, new links so bookmarked pages still function.

One way that some of our clients have retained their "old site" is to provide a link to an archived version of their original site. This archived version then lists the correct updated page, giving the website visitors an opportunity to update their bookmarks and visit your most recently edited page.

Tip 12
Make it Simple, Keep it Real

The more complex and cluttered your website is, the harder time your visitor has when she visits.

Keep it simple. Take some extra time to review your content from a new visitor's perspective. Common business website issues for the general public include:

1) **industry-specific jargon** that a non-initiate would not understand (if your site is targeted to people who would understand your lexicon, by all means, stick to it; if you're reaching out to people not familiar with your industry, at least add a glossary page)

2) **alphabet soup**, with many abbreviations or acronyms that only specialists understand (just because you refer to it does not mean your customer understands it)

3) **cryptic navigation** (test your site on people outside of your industry: if they find the navigation confusing, rework it

so it's more straightforward)

4) **too many words** (you don't need to explain your entire procedure when only a few phrases, some well-placed diagrams, or an image will suffice)

5) **not enough information** (your website is part of your sales team, so make it work just like a salesperson. Provide lists of features and benefits, offer internet specials, and add a buy now button.)

6) **no call to action** (if your website doesn't inform visitors of their next steps, they will not know what to do next. Explain their next step!)

7) **correct contact information** (add your correct contact information to each page so visitors know how to find you)

Give your potential customers enough web-based information so they easily and naturally take the next step to saying yes to you and your services.

Summary to Keep in Mind: Website Basics

Keep in mind that your visitors consider your website a physical, literal interpretation of who you are: how they interact with the website is how they expect to do business with you.

Budget adequately for your web development process, including the costs of maintaining and continuing to fine-tune your website. Take time to review and prepare well-written, clear content so anyone who visits knows exactly what you offer. Make your design "fit" your style of work and your industry. Include pictures and biographies of key people in your organization to establish credentials. Respect the user's time, and make sure the site loads quickly into the browser.

Keep your web content easy to view and simple to use, reducing emphasis on interactive elements unless you need these items for your target audience.

As you get more feedback from visitors and users, provide new functionality or new features to streamline your business process, and offer continually updated content pages such as blogs, picture galleries, samples, or articles.

Prominently post your privacy policy and any company policies. Keep your contact information updated and provide "signposts" along the way to direct visitor traffic.

If you anticipate doing a redesign, consider updating your website's "look" once a year at most, because too much change may be disconcerting to repeat visitors.

Keep your website content simple and "real" to begin a process that helps your customer or community member understand you. Doing so will keep customers loyal to your website, your products, your services, and your company.

Chapter 2: Share Your Knowledge

- Why Share? Reasons Why Giving is Good
- 13. Blog it: Be an Authority in your Field
- 14. Calendar It: Display Relevant Industry Events
- 15. White Papers: Create an Online Brain Trust
- 16. Interactive Items: Add Calculators and Estimators for Sticky Effect
- 17. Dig Deep: Provide "Ask the Expert" Pages
- 18. Make it Fun: Add a Quiz or Poll
- 19. Control Junk E-mail: Create an Opt-in List
- 20. You're Linked In: Be an Answer Provider
- 21. Forums: Provide Answers for your Community
- 22. Placement: Add a Link to your Signature
- 23. Lighten Up: Humor Makes Visitors Happy
- 24. Be a Good Guest Host: Network and Share
- Summary to Keep in Mind: Share your Knowledge

Why Share? Reasons Why Giving is Good

I recommend that you share your knowledge on your website as a way to gain trust, earn referrals, and encourage "buy-in" from your customers. Here are three reasons to share your knowledge online:

1) When you give away your knowledge, you demonstrate that you stand in a position of strength. For example, offering a series of free "how-to" articles or displaying a typical process checklist positions you as an expert who radiates honesty, forthrightness, and trust. You have everything to gain when you share your mastery of your field.

2) When you give away your knowledge, you receive much more in return. Reciprocity is a well-known part of our human nature. When you give away, you receive back.

3) My theory is that when you share resource articles and insider information about your industry, you benefit from opportunities from current and new customers. You attract interest from potential partners and supporters who see that they can benefit from associating with you. You also provide information that benefits your

entire field and raises the standard for those operating in your industry.

When you give away your knowledge, you build your reputation, which converts to client confidence and trust in your integrity. This is the best kind of social capital.

When you find ways to share your knowledge online, you build your business and your personal reputation. Remain transparent, demonstrate integrity, and share wisely.

Tip 13
Blog it: Be an Authority in your Field

What is a Blog?
A blog, or web log, displays entries in reverse chronological order (such as in a journal or diary). Blogs provide commentary, opinions, insights, or news. Blogs may cover any subject such as food, politics, new electronic gadgets, or environmental issues. Some personal blogs function as online diaries.

A typical corporate blog combines text and images and links to other blogs, web pages and media. Blogs also include ways for others to comment on specific entries. The majority of blogs display text, although some focus primarily on photographs (photo blogs), videos (v-logs), or audio (podcasting). The word "blog" may also be used as a verb, meaning to add content to a blog ("Have Kelly do a blog post about the product release today.")

Why Bother with a Blog?
A blog is easy to update and keeps you very current. Use your blog to create an informative, useful, and timely net that fishes out information, news, views, and opinions in your field. You are the

fisherwoman who identifies the "catch" and you haul in the stories.

Give readers meaningful explanations about your company by using blog posts to share your expertise. Put yourself in great demand for services, products, and speaking or writing gigs as you post more quality blog items on your field of expertise, guest post on other blogs, promote new products and services, or highlight an interesting new initiative. HINT: Do NOT post relentless commercial messages to your blog. They're not meaningful or engaging at all.

Developing the Blog

Some hosting companies offer a one-step installation of open source, free blog software. You may contact any web professional for a quote on installing Wordpress on your own host, so the blog name is www.yourwebsite.com/blog. You may also want to sign up for a popular Blogspot or Typepad account, where your blog is hosted on their servers and the blog address is yourblog.blogspot.com.

How do I Write a Post?

Use your assigned login and password to the administrator section of your blog. You'll land on a main "dashboard" with all your available options, such as publishing posts, publishing pages, updating the look and feel of the site, and managing subscribers and comments. A "post" appears in your blog section. A permanent "page" appears in your navigation section. Practice and see what happens! You always have the option to delete a page or post.

What do I Write About?

Your blog content typically focuses on your particular theme with periodic mention of your business, news in the industry, or behind-the-scenes information on product releases. I highly recommend that you visit other content-specific blogs to see how other posts are created (my blog, www.Sistersinbiz.com, focuses on women of color in business).

Write your post from your own point of view, and make it engaging, relevant, or thought-provoking. However, your readers don't need to know the latest details of your personal life (relationships, shopping, pets, children) unless they are relevant to your company. Also, refrain from an excess of "corporate speak" or highly self-promoting blogging.

Use multiple sources for inspiration, ideas, events, industry trends, and other "blog fodder," including:

- Daily or weekly news in your target area
- Your business process
- News that affects your industry or your clients
- Books, articles or magazines you're reading
- Events that you attend, organize, or lead
- Events from associations or membership groups
- Initiatives within your company
- Charitable drives, auctions, or events
- Other blogs in your content area (do a web search on "Blog on _____" and fill in your topic area)
- How-to articles
- Articles specific to your readers' interests

Blogging Tips

I typically break down my blog posts into *appetizers* and *entrées*. "Appetizers" are small portions of information, conveniently organized for both search engines and readers, that may be devoured in five minutes. Consider formats such as Top Ten Lists, Thought of the Day, Tip of the Week, Highlight of the Month, Memorable Quote, My

Resource List, or Weekly Roundup. Post these informational tidbits on a regular basis.

"Entrées" are longer pieces, typically between 1500 - 2500 words, that delve into a specific topic. These take longer to think about, write, and digest, but they routinely become your most frequently visited and most frequently linked pages. Consider doing an ongoing series of blog posts, all on the same topic, and spread the posts out over a week or two.

Maintain different categories of information so your readers may browse through different posts based on their own interests. Utilize particular keywords within your post that help with website search engines. For example, a blog on green businesses includes keywords like LOHAS, green, "reduce, reuse, recycle," water conservation, environmental sustainability, carbon neutral, solar power, organic, or other tags.

What to Avoid!
Refrain from copying and pasting blog posts that are copyrighted by another author. Do not post shoddily researched posts. Practice politeness. Good blog "netiquette" means refraining from offensive posts. Be vigilant about doing "hard selling" of your

product or service. While there are definitely things to avoid, there are many things to embrace on your blog. Consider writing about your opinions on the larger environment of your field, upcoming trends in your industry, introductions to key players, interviews with decision makers, reports that you've researched, and new developments that affect your clients or readers.

Some additional advice would be to upload your own photos to your own server rather than "hot linking" to someone else's image, add a catchy title to each blog post, add a 'related posts' section to keep your readers interested and involved with the topic and include stock quotes, biographies, logos, or links when you refer to them.

Your Blog is your Home on the Web: Make it Comfortable
Keep your posts lively, and make your viewpoint clear. Let readers hear "your voice." Avoid creating another boring technobabble or jargon-encrusted blog or one lacking original content. A blog is your home on the web: keep it clean and tidy, and make sure your visitors will want to visit you again.

Invite readers to bookmark your blog posts (www.addthis.com) or to subscribe to your blog's "feed" (www.feedburner.com) so they receive entries via e-mail. Comment on the blogs of other authors, adding additional information or expanding commentary as you see fit. You'll make great friends and develop a community of like-minded people all working on the issues that are important to you and your business. Finally, your blog posts will end up cached in the search engines. Monitor what is being published, stand by your posts, fact-check, and keep your blog up-to-date.

As a final word of advice: your blog represents your unique viewpoint. When you maintain it with regular postings and a unique, active voice, you provide perspective and assistance to your readers. Each blog post functions as a separate page of content for your website. Use these expanded web pages to increase your website search rankings.

Not every company benefits from a business-related blog, but if you or someone on your team is available to participate as a regular writer (at least once a week), do consider using the blog to increase your website's reach. Ideally, you have three items in place: the capacity to maintain the blog, a point of view that enhances your company's reputation as a helpful resource, and a plan for regular posting. If you have these items in place, add a company blog onto your corporate website as soon as possible.

Checklists for improving your blog:

Is your blog/Does your blog:
☐ Laid out in an intuitive and easy-to-understand way?
☐ Offer links to archived posts by date?
☐ Offer links to archived posts by category?
☐ List an "About the Author" page with details?
☐ Reference your company website when appropriate?
☐ Offer search capability?
☐ Include a "blogroll" or list of links to related sites?

Does your blog post:
☐ Cover a trend, news item, development, event, or key player within the blog topic of interest?
☐ Display an informative title?
☐ Appear well-researched, timely, useful?
☐ Include relevant keywords? Include related posts?
☐ Include a picture, table, or chart for visual interest?
☐ Contain clear, fact-checked links?

☐ Consist of only your own materials or clearly states any links to other authors' works?
☐ Omit offensive, inflammatory material?

In addition, did you:
☐ Spell-check?
☐ Grammar check?
☐ Check punctuation?
☐ Fact check?
☐ Edit for clarity?
☐ Add related topics, hyperlinks, or relevant images?
☐ Sign your name or personalize your post?
☐ Add a link to your company, if desired?

Tip 14
Calendar It:
Display Relevant Industry Events

Create a calendar as a go-to reference for relevant events in your field. Because of information overload and the openness of the Internet, web visitors appreciate when you filter, synthesize, and sort all the available events into a concise "must-attend" list. Such a calendar will help your visitors keep abreast of local or Internet-based events. These may be networking events, informational seminars, speaker panels, conventions, book readings, work parties, volunteer opportunities, or other gatherings.

Use a calendar to organize your own work schedule and allow time for at least one networking event per month. For example, if you've been invited to speak on a panel, schedule this into your web calendar so web visitors know where they may find you. They might not actually attend, but your visitors will at least know your availability. If your company offers its own events or you require RSVPs, consider adding an 'RSVP online' option to your calendar.

Real-life examples of web calendars include an annual list of craft fairs where a jewelry maker intends to show her work, a list of the most important home decor conventions for a furniture accents supplier, a calendar of upcoming conventions for a grassroots political group, and a list of annual gatherings for professionals in your industry.

Checklist for what to include in your calendar:
- [ ] Start date and end date
- [ ] Start time/s and end time/s
- [ ] Title of event
- [ ] Short description of event
- [ ] Contact person for the event
- [ ] Informational website link, if any
- [ ] Prices for organizational members
- [ ] Prices for the general public
- [ ] RSVP online, if available
- [ ] Calendar in grid format or in list format
- [ ] Consistent display for events

Tip 15
White Papers:
Create an Online Brain Trust

In some fields, you provide a valuable service when you offer up-to-date information. A delay of even a month on time-sensitive data may mean a different outcome to someone's business. Consider offering white papers as background research to web visitors who may need highly specific information to make an informed decision. While you need not add proprietary code, trade secrets, or private information, you may add facts, figures, graphs, charts, preliminary studies, or research papers on your field.

Query experts in related fields to provide information that will help your consumer make a better decision. For example, a graphic designer may offer a printer's perspective on styles, paper stock, quantities, color options, and document preparation for printing. A food website offers professional chef recipes, food styling tips, or restaurant reviews. A baby products website offers parents' reviews or parenting articles.

When you offer a library of reading material, downloadable samples, or even mini-versions of your full product, your potential customers can evaluate the quality and relevance of your resources to their needs. Use HTML, PDF, Flash, or other well-known formats to make sure your files display the way you intend.

Add a section of "recent reports" to your homepage or to a downloads page. The content within your website must be your company's original content, and you must have permission (if needed) to distribute it. Protect your company by adding your logo, the paper's author, and a watermark, if desired.

Tip 16
Interactive Items: Add Calculators and Estimators for Sticky Effect

If your work requires an estimate that you give to a client in order to proceed, consider offering a quote generator or an online calculator.

For example, in the website development business, an easy rule of thumb is to estimate the cost based on the complexity of the design, the number of pages, and the functional modules desired. Fixed costs include the domain and hosting. In this case, an estimate calculator will help a potential customer determine the cost of her proposed website. The customer can also change variables to see how different choices impact the final estimate for her project.

Financial services companies, mortgage firms, banks, and any company that deals with figures may offer online calculators to help web visitors understand the factors involved in finding their "magic number." These tools make your customers' discovery process easier. Offer as much as possible to help customers understand your pricing *before* they connect with you in person or over the phone.

Checklist for interactive calculators/estimators:

☐ Do you offer job-based or fixed pricing? If so, show your calculations for greater transparency.

☐ If not, do you offer a "Frequently Asked Questions" page for potential customers to understand your process or rates?

☐ If you offer quotes, do you have an online estimate generator or a costs calculator?

☐ Can customers change variables to check for different options?

☐ Can customers e-mail their results to you?

☐ Can customers e-mail their results to themselves for easy reference?

☐ Make sure there is no sign-up or login information necessary to request a quote, unless you require this information

Tip 17
Dig Deep:
Provide "Ask the Expert" Pages

Whether you consider yourself an expert or not, if you're in business, you're providing deep knowledge and skills in a particular content area. This knowledge qualifies you as an expert! When you use your website to share your expertise, you provide a genuine resource to both current and potential customers.

An easy way to share is to offer a column or regularly updated section comprising frequently asked questions and your answers, tools, or recommendations.

For example, a column entitled, "Ask the Interior Decorator" may contain a section with design tips for challenging spaces. "Ask the Painter" may offer recommendations on colors, paint brands, or tools. "Ask the Financial Expert" may display your particular expertise on stock picks, market trends, industry information, or retirement-related concerns. "Ask the Vet" may offer breeder-specific or animal-specific answers.

Because people who are visiting your website want to know your general "tone" and personality, use this section to promote your expertise. Help your visitors decide if you are the one they want to hire for their specific project.

Furthermore, if you are on the receiving end of many similar questions, answer them in your "Ask the Expert" page and give your visitor a place to begin her conversation with you. An "Ask the Expert" component will enhance the efficiency of your website and save your visitors time, as well.

Some businesses may use this section to further specify their particular type of client. For example, if you do kitchen remodels in a particular price range, this section is a great opportunity to mention that range and further specify if the website visitor "fits" your own target client list.

Checklist for sections that share expertise:
- [ ] Credentials clearly established?
- [ ] Content within the section updated regularly?
- [ ] Visitors may submit a question to the expert?
- [ ] Additional contact information as needed
- [ ] May customers contact the expert directly?
- [ ] List any disclaimers or policies to protect the expert advisor

Tip 18
Make it Fun: Add a Quiz or Poll

Polls and quizzes add levity and a bit of entertainment to the typically tedious task of searching for a vendor online. Your quiz may be a way for visitors to "see how much they know" about your industry, with two to five questions that you'd like to ask. Your poll provides a way for you to gauge a response to your own questions. For example, for a site focused on product software, you might provide a poll asking what version users are currently using.

Make sure your quiz, poll, or questionnaire adds value to your site. If it's relevant, sheds more light on your service, provides quick information to other visitors, or gives you information about who is visiting, use it on your website.

Make sure your quiz or poll does not require registration (if you want people to actually participate). If you choose to require an e-mail address, add that input form after the participant has answered the quiz. No one wants to be badgered into participating, so make sure your quiz is welcoming and user-friendly. Only use multiple-choice or true/false answers, as open-ended questions may become unruly to collect and display. Offer a way for participants to view all the answers, typically after they've answered the question.

An interactive module like your poll or quiz is a fun way to gain insight from your visitors. Remember to update your questions on a regular basis!

Checklist for polls, quizzes, or questionnaires:
- [ ] Update polls or other interactive features on a regular basis?
- [ ] Your poll or quiz does not require personal information to participate
- [ ] Decide if visitors may view results without participating?
- [ ] Graphs or charts as needed, to show the outcome of a poll
- [ ] Questions are true/false or multiple-choice?

Tip 19
Control Junk E-Mail: Create an Opt-in List

Most people prefer to spend time with their family and friends, pursue important activities, or get real work done instead of dealing with junk e-mail. What constitutes junk e-mail? In my view, junk mail consists of any of the following:

>1) e-mail for which the recipient did not sign up
>2) e-mail from which the recipient cannot unsubscribe
>3) e-mail without a link to the original site sending it

If you dislike junk mail as much as I do (and if you receive as much as I do in a typical day, you definitely dislike it), you'll take extra precautions to insure that all your e-mail communications find a happy response upon their delivery.

E-mail communications form a large part of normal interactions with a company, so it's best to start off asking permission if you may send e-mail to your users. This involves an opt-in process: users submit their contact information and confirm that they have opted to receive communications from you. It's always thoughtful to offer links to your latest e-newsletters so visitors may preview what they will actually receive.

When you have legitimate news that benefits your clients, readers, or website visitors or if you offer a service that's timely and truly of interest to your mailing list, then feel good about sending your message to your community. It helps members feel like they're "in the know" and have access to behind-the-scenes information.

I always recommend developing a list of people who truly care about your products and services and who want to hear from you, as opposed to a "ho-hum" list of people who don't actually enjoy receiving your e-mail missive and who will delete it or, worse, spam filter it upon arrival.

When you send out messages, always make sure that you offer an opt-out link in the bottom part of the newsletter. Also, offer a link to your visitors so they can change their e-mail address, update their own contact information, or even choose which types of announcements they'd like to receive.

When you control junk e-mail, offer opt-ins and unsubscribe links, and truly target the message that you send, you keep your business active in the eyes of the people who care the most. Through your e-mail list, you're building a loyal base of fans who enjoy hearing from you. Respect the trust they place in you and maintain the newsletter as a valuable service. You build one of your most important assets with your permission-based e-mail list.

I recommend minimizing the number of e-mails you send. Is your message so important that people must hear from you every day? If you offer a regular service, then you're fine (e.g. Sunfire NewsWire offers a daily roundup of Asian-American news); but if you're simply sending promotional messages, consider sending messages only on a monthly, quarterly, or special seasonal basis.

Proofread your announcement, and always consider the question of "so what?" You've crafted your newsletter, so what? Before pressing the "send" button, confirm that your newsletter truly increases the quality of your business relationship. If you plan on sending e-mail, make sure your recipient cares. Otherwise, they'll say "so what?" and delete or unsubscribe.

Tip 20
You're Linked In: Be an Answer Provider

The professional networking service, LinkedIn.com, continues to grow in usability and value, and the current "Questions and Answers" section provides insight into current trends in specific industries.

For example, recruiters post their tips on how to find qualified applicants; people with heavy involvement in new technologies answer specific, obscure, or technical questions; and people recommend services with which they have experience. It's a great source of up-to-date information.

If you're an answer provider or you have some knowledge in a particular field, share your knowledge by answering other people's questions. You might do this on LinkedIn or on a different service like a forum, bulletin board, or listserv that's related to your company.

When you build up social capital by answering questions in a helpful way, you easily make connections for potential sales. More importantly, you build your reputation as someone other people trust. While I don't recommend you dominate a bulletin board with your answers or take over a forum posting with links back to your website, I do recommend you find online networks of people interested in your field and contribute to other people's questions and answers. If you're thoughtful, knowledgeable, and demonstrate integrity, your reputation (or at least your search results) as an answer provider will spread. When it does come time to select a vendor, your bulletin board mates may be more inclined to choose you over a competitor.

Checklist for participating in Q&A sessions:
- [ ] Add thoughtful answers that demonstrate your mastery of subject matter
- [ ] Refrain from one-word or one-line answers
- [ ] Contribute to a discussion
- [ ] Stay away from "flame wars" or rude posters
- [ ] Maintain a respectful tone
- [ ] Add your contact information or motto
- [ ] Offer longer or more in-depth answers offline

Tip 21
Forums: Provide Answers for your Community

Online forums function like community information centers: people post and respond on topics of interest. For some forums a user must register and wait for approval before posting; for others, users may post anonymously. Certain members of an online forum may be assigned as "moderators" with the privilege of banning or deleting users or postings that don't fit the forum's guidelines for activity.

The great thing about forums is that they will typically allow you to visit as a "lurker," simply reading but not responding, until you work up enough courage or interest to share your viewpoint by commenting or starting a new "thread" of discussion.

When you become involved in a forum that truly interests you, you'll discover new friends, often times from around the world, who share your interest. The forums available on the Web today cover every conceivable topic, so you'll probably be able to find an online community focusing on a narrow topic like Filipina businesswomen, Indian ring-necked parakeets, or even green living in Portland (all topics of interest to me).

If you don't find your community, ask your web developer to install forum software on your own site, and create your own community as one of the founders!

Use online communities to participate with other people hooked into your field of interest. I've been participating online in one alumni group for more than five years and have seen my own development within the group, from seeking jobs and requesting mentors to posting jobs and advising younger graduates. You'll make friends and find potential customers online at your local forum. Use it!

Tip 22
Placement: Add a Link to your Signature

One of the easiest ways to promote your business is to add your name, title, contact information, and a tag line to your outgoing e-mail. This is how mine reads:

Monica S. Flores, Principal
10K Webdesign
http://www.10kwebdesign.com
website design :: business solutions
minority owned, woman owned, green certified

Add your phone number, e-mail address, and postal mail address, as desired. I also add a link to my LinkedIn profile, and you might consider adding a blog page, Facebook page, or other social networking tool that matches your business model.

When contact information is added to your signature, correspondents easily connect with you. Potential customers can connect with you if they've seen your e-mail on a listserv or your message was forwarded from a friend. What's more, a tag line, motto, or additional keywords give e-mail correspondents an easy way to assess if your business fits their current needs. Think of a 7 second "memory hook" to match your business, and add that to your signature box for all outgoing e-mail.

Checklist for using your signature consistently:
☐ Contact information attached to out-going messages
☐ Your tag line acts as a "memory hook" for potential e-mail correspondents?
☐ Add your public profile if it fits your business model (LinkedIn, MySpace, YouTube, Twitter, your blog, etc.)
☐ Make sure your contact information is correct and all phone numbers, fax numbers, e-mail addresses, and links function!

Tip 23
Lighten Up:
Humor Makes Visitors Happy

Humor, if used judiciously, goes a long way towards entertaining your visitors and letting them know more about you and your company's sense of fun, humor, playfulness, or creativity.

If your site does not benefit from humor, then please disregard this tip; but if your site does allow an opportunity for you to provide a respite for today's busy, left-brain-focused worker, take it. There's a reason newspaper readers open up the Sunday Funnies section first and magazine readers go to the back page to see the silly picture or the comical illustration.

Some ideas for a humorous section to add to your website include: "Humor at Work," "Funny Stories from the Field," "Joke of the Week," "Picture of the Month," or "Overheard in the Office." You might also include items like bloopers, "easter eggs" (hidden messages), or "Stories from our Customers" to provide more insight into your company or organizational "vibe."

Many of your web visitors will appreciate your sense of humor if it gives them better insight into a potential working relationship with you. Use your judgement.

Checklist for humorous content:
☐ Is your website a banking, financial, or legal site? If so, be very careful about using humor on your website.
☐ Is your site zany, irreverent, creative, or whimsical?
If so, consider adding:
    ☐ Funny stories
    ☐ Jokes or silly situations
    ☐ "Overheard" dialogue
    ☐ Funny, entertaining pictures
☐ Disallow off-topic or off-putting humor
☐ Add disclaimers and notices, if needed
☐ Make sure that all humor is tasteful and appropriate!

Tip 24
Be a Good Guest Host: Network and Share

Your website is your home on the web where you will continuously act as hostess to numerous visitors, interested parties, and passers-by who visit you online. Consider ways in which you may extend hospitality to other people in your field of interest by knowing how to be a good guest, too!

My biggest recommendation for networking is, in the words of Dante, *from a little spark may burst a mighty flame.* To me, this means that you participate, help, and find ways to provide value to the people with whom you work online. All of us working together truly make a larger difference. For example, if a well-known blogger invites you to provide a guest post for her, add a link to this fact on your own website, and invite your own readers to participate with comments. If you're tasked with providing online content for your membership group's e-newsletter, consider ways to write a fresh, informative, and useful article, such as a Top Ten list that's relevant to the news today. Your colleagues appreciate your effort. If you're in charge of press releases, compile a list of public relations specialists who benefit from being "in the know" about news in your specific industry, and send them any groundbreaking initiatives that your company undertakes.

Be a good guest when you're part of the overall network that makes up the World Wide Web, and you'll find yourself learning how to be a gentle, influential, and persuasive host, too. This approach will translate into a bigger bottom line for your own ideas, products, and services. You'll also have opportunities to draw from a larger pool of people willing to share with you because of the many times you have participated and shared as a guest on their projects.

To make it easier to share your information, compile the following into a page and post it prominently on your website:

- your contact information
- your headshot in JPG format at web-ready 72 dpi resolution and print-ready 300 dpi resolution
- a 3-paragraph biography
- a summary of you and your services
- a collection of your quotes
- any supporting information such as licensing, degrees, awards, or accolades

Summary to Keep in Mind: Share your Knowledge

Reciprocity means that when you share your knowledge about your field, your generosity will return in many ways, from business opportunities, to write-ups and positive reviews, to recommendations, and to more sales. I have found that any kind of pro bono, volunteer, reduced price, or sharing-related work that I engage in comes back to me in the form of additional contacts, additional opportunities to bid on projects, and a good reputation.

Sharing is easy. Because you know so much about your unique field of interest, simply seek out ways to present this knowledge and speak with authority on the topic: use your own blog, a forum posting, or a question-and-answer service. On your website, consider increasing the customer-centric resources you provide, like a calendar of upcoming events, a downloadable set of research papers about your field, online calculators, an "Ask the Expert" page, or polls and quizzes relevant to your industry. Finally, consider ways to share your knowledge as both an online and offline "guest," as well as a "host."

Sharing, caring, and being connected to a larger community all increase our own sense of participation. Share your own expertise and experience. Talk about what you do best. This may be your interest in your own business, your specific part of a larger process, or your own treasured hobby or activity. When you give some things away for free, your generosity will translate into bigger net profits for your business.

As an example, I was asked to host a presentation for a woman's business group. As a followup to the presentation, I posted the materials for the presentation to my website. These included the original PowerPoint file, which I uploaded to Slideshare.net (where you may upload PPT or PDF files). I also uploaded a PDF of the main conference handout, some sample files to download, screenshots from recommended links, and a more comprehensive resource guide. Each of these pieces of information adds to the general knowledge base available to your clients and gives you an opportunity to "cover" housekeeping or basics, freeing you up to focus on what you do best. Posting the information also offers an opportunity to update your "What's New" page.

I recommend you revisit your Ideal Website Flow document and mark additional steps on how you will keep content fresh by adding materials like those listed above. If you are currently not participating in sharing-related situations such as panel presentations or seminars, you may still upload your personal knowledge, business processes, or research project findings using the principal of reciprocation.

I promise you that it works! Give something away, and you'll receive something back.

Chapter 3: Build a Resource List

- Be a Resource to your Customers
- 25. You're a Clearinghouse: Link to Subject Matter
- 26. Show your Trust: Provide Referral Links
- 27. Share Links: High Quality Means High Results
- Summary to Keep in Mind: Build a Resource List

Be a Resource to your Customers

When we focus on building up our business, we sometimes get bogged down in the operations, the constant challenges, and the problems. However, when we take a step back and look at the big picture, we realize that any business is all about its customers. With no customers, there are no sales; and with no sales, there's zip, zero, zilch, nada, nothing. When you embrace this fundamental aspect of building your company, you realize that providing "customer love" must be your most important focus, both in your website and in your person-to-person interactions.

Offer resources galore for both your existing clients and visitors. Your thoughtfulness shows that you appreciate and support your customers. Casual visitors will turn into your favorite customers based on your fabulous customer service!

Resources may be people, things, or information:

When you provide resource **people**, you offer links to other individuals, groups, or organizations that you feel comfortable recommending and whom you think your customers will benefit from contacting.

When you provide resource **things**, you supply actual physical tools, gadgets, or items that help your customers solve their problems, help them feel better or more productive, and give them ways to live better lives.

When you provide resource **information**, you provide answers to solve an existing need that your customers may or may not verbalize. Your ability to provide targeted resource information proves that you listen and that you keep your customers' best interests at heart. Improve your customer care by focusing on how to be a useful resource to them.

In today's micro-specific business world, when you identify and dominate your particular sphere of influence, you become even more of a resource to those involved in your field. Identify your niche and specific field of interest. Then become synonymous with that field of interest.

For example, I am passionate about educating, empowering, and connecting women of color, particularly minority women using business as a vehicle for personal and professional growth. I am also supportive of progressive, green, and socially responsible businesses.

Because of my interests and my sphere of influence, most of my clients self-identify with one or more of the above descriptors. I also receive opportunities to provide book reviews or product reviews on items that fit these categories. My blog receives targeted advertising on these keywords (minority, women, business, social responsibility). I post original articles on these subjects. Finally, I derive great pleasure from meeting others who hold interests similar to my own.

When you identify your own company or organizational niche, you begin to increase your "reach" into the target community within that niche. Your website is a great place to start that process.

As you build up your resource list, your customers trust you more, and your potential partners, affiliates, sponsors, and advertisers gain better ways to work with you and support your work.

Tip 25
You're a Clearinghouse: Link to Subject Matter

Subject matter changes quickly as knowledge grows in a particular field. Today's information worker processes hundreds of pieces of information in a month from newspapers, radio, television, and internet usage. As a result of the ever-expanding knowledge base in the world, your reputation as someone "in the know" helps your customers and clients trust your judgement.

Act as a clearinghouse of select information by incorporating the following into your industry:

- Articles in the news that directly impact your clients
- Editorials on trends in your industry
- Tools such as software or physical objects being released in your field
- Upcoming or expected government regulation in your field
- Policy changes that impact your company
- International trends or agreements that impact clients

- Emerging trends that your customers may not know
- Scenarios or potential situations that your customers should be aware of

As you add up-to-date information on your industry, others will view your site as a trusted information source. Arrange your site in a way that highlights your abilities to share multiple pieces of information that affect your clients.

I recommend adding a "Resources" section that you categorize by tool or by subject matter. Maintain this resources section with up-to-date resource links, and encourage your website visitors to bookmark you and send you "tips."

Tip 26
Show your Trust: Provide Referral Links

When people trust you, you are one step ahead of any other vendor they have in mind. Trust forms the basis of many relationships, and the mutually beneficial relationship that customers and providers share depends on trust.

I recommend you take some time during your business planning process every year to develop an "Ideal Client Template" of your desired customers. When you do this, you make it easier and faster to identify and "sort" the people you'll potentially serve.

• Is your lead an ideal client or would they be better served somewhere else?
• Who is your client?
• What types of issues do they deal with on a daily basis?
• How do they feel?
• How will you assist them?
• Where do they live and work?
• What's their typical challenge in their workplace?
• What is their primary role?
• What would make their performance better?

As you develop a snapshot of your ideal client, you will be more specific about your own customer policies; and as you develop more clarity, you'll find allies who naturally refer these clients to you. With whom do you typically work as a natural fit to your own business? Identify your associates, and develop your circle of connectors to branch out into a wider world of potential customers.

For example, a circle of people who naturally refer business to each other includes a financial planner, an estate-planning attorney, a CPA or enrolled agent, a life insurance salesperson, a real estate agent, a mortgage specialist, a health insurance specialist, and a professional coach or trainer. If you are one of these types of people, you will want to develop your own circle of connectors. Find one or two solid, trustworthy professionals in each of these fields. As you work together, you will find that you provide better service and meet more people through sharing books of business. As you develop a tight group of people who look out for one other, share leads, and provide specific types of assistance to specific types of clients, all of you will provide a higher level of service because the transition from one professional to the next is smooth.

Here are some ideas for organizations where you will meet and find your own circle of connectors:

- BNI (Business Network International)
- NAWBO (National Association of Women Business Owners) and other women's groups
- Topical groups or trade associations
- Alumni associations
- Sports teams, art clubs, or garden groups
- Volunteer boards or community events
- Places of worship, if you already attend
- Moms' groups or parents' groups
- Other hobby-related groups

I also recommend you visit social networking sites:
- LinkedIn www.linkedin.com
- Facebook www.facebook.com
- Meetup www.meetup.com

Joining a person-to-person group gives you a good way to mingle on- and offline with people who share your common interests. Some of your connections may result in business transactions, so keep looking to build a wide-ranging network of associates.

As you build your list of recommendations, consider posting this "recommended list" in a special section of your website. You may offer a resource directory or a list of links with contact information, a brief description, and an explanation of why you recommend this person.

When you share your recommended list with others, you build up both your associates' trust factor (and search engine results) as well as your own. Keep your list separate from any affiliate links or "paid postings," because you add much more value to your recommendations list when you have nothing to gain from it except your reputation as a good source of referrals.

In my experience, our lead generation time reduces drastically based on any referrals we receive from another party (usually a former client or someone who has first-hand knowledge about our web development skills). By our third year in business, the majority of our clients were referred to us by one of our trusted partners or past customers, and most of our clients came to us ready to hire us for their own website project.

Bottom line, your list of links shows that you trust others and that they trust you, and your referral to a trusted provider means worlds to your potential customer (ask anyone who's needed an emergency dentist!). So, share your knowledge!

Checklist for providing helpful referral links:
- [ ] Add a resource directory of referral links to associates
- [ ] Add referral links to professionals in your city or county
- [ ] Referral links include up-to-date contact information
- [ ] Include web links, descriptions, or testimonials
- [ ] Ask permission of associates before linking to them
- [ ] Update annually so contact information stays current
- [ ] Keep "paid" or "sponsored" links different from referral links

Tip 27
Share Links:
High Quality means High Results

Search engine listings typically count the number of incoming and outgoing links from your pages. When your page has hundreds or thousands of incoming links, search engines add a level of "authority" to your web page: this level increases your page ranking in search results. Check your Technorati.com rating for a sample.

Exchange links with other high-quality websites to promote your company. When you exchange a link with another website owner, check the accuracy of the link and spell-check the descriptive text. Refrain from posting on "splogs" (fake blogs) or on sites that primarily consist of unrelated links or paid links. These do not assist your page ranking.

When you consider linking with another site, think quality over quantity. A well-placed link from another high-ranking website means much more than a number of links from poorly-ranked websites. Pass on any opportunities that involve "shady" subjects, companies with which you don't want to be involved, or topical areas you prefer to decline.

If you find your website linked to a page with questionable content, politely ask the webmaster to remove your link. On the other hand, if you desire a link from a website with very high-quality content and high page rankings, ask nicely, consider ways to promote that website that benefit both of you, or find ways to make the outgoing link to your site worth the site owner's effort.

Some ways to add links are to develop relationships with high-ranked bloggers or authority figures within your niche market, to join a "web ring" or list of links shared by multiple websites within a particular subject, or to specifically ask the contact person of the website with whom you wish to be affiliated.

Remember to be sweet, and you'll get more sweetness in return!

Summary to Keep in Mind: Build a Resource List

When you provide high-quality content, you invest in your site and you make sure your site is link-worthy. Remember to target your niche customers by using keywords within your text that emphasize your particular specialty, by providing relevant, useful, and timely information on your website, and by maintaining multiple links to other resources.

You offer a terrific service to your website visitors when you add lists of resources, a directory of links, or a referral directory. Visitors learn all about your business, and they also have the opportunity to learn about the company you keep (your referral and recommendation lists). Maintain up-to-date, relevant incoming links and updated outgoing links to your recommended associates. As you continue to add these resource links, you'll grow your status as a resource provider, and you'll benefit from organic searches by people using your target keywords.

Some real-life examples of high quality linking ideas follow:

A political candidate links to other candidates she supports, as well as to candidates who have endorsed her campaign. She links to groups that back her candidacy. She also offers links to local election boards, includes a link on how to register to vote, and lists all the party groups within her target area. She links to community groups, grassroots groups, citizen advocacy groups, schools, hospitals, and clinics in her geographical range, while providing links to existing city and state government. Finally, she offers a list of businesses in the area, organized by category.

A massage therapist offers links to allied health care providers with whom she works, including a local dentist, a chiropractor, an acupuncturist, a midwife, a therapist, a coach, a naturopath, a physician, a nutritionist, and a health foods store. She recommends these professionals with their contact information, a description of their specialty, and her reasons for referring clients. She adds links to the causes she supports and the non-profit for which she serves as board member. She also adds links to local professionals that she works with and that her clients are using, such as nannies, child care centers, attorneys, insurance agents, financial planners, and other service providers.

A community directory for a neighborhood provides a members-only directory for businesses, non-profit organizations, individuals, and services in that postal code. Residents may use the business directory to find and support local businesses, get assistance for household or community needs, and find others within their neighborhood or block.

A "mommy blog" author offers her own high-quality content about working at home. She does frequent reviews of products that relate to babies, toddlers, children, and adolescents. She maintains a link list of other stay-at-home-mom and work-at-home-mom bloggers, and she offers sponsored reviews of services that relate to mothers and parents. She links to pregnancy resources, and she offers a geographical directory, organized by state, of midwives, doulas, lactation consultants, and parenting groups. Each of these sites link back to her website.

The above examples show some of the infinite ways to use link building to increase your website presence. When you focus on quality, provide reciprocal links, and consider linking only to other well-linked sites, you'll increase your website page ranking. You'll also increase your status as a resource provider in your chosen field of work.

Chapter 4:
Target your Clients

- Finding the Right People Means Focusing
- 28. Be Personable: Meet People Online and Offline
- 29. Use Social Networking: An Overview
- 30. Show, Don't Tell: Add a Demonstration
- 31. Comment Thoughtfully on Other Sites
- 32. Are you Legitimate? Add Testimonials
- 33. Photo Gallery: Provide Samples of your Work
- 34. Share your Values: Report on your Vision
- Summary to Keep in Mind: Target your Clients

Finding the Right People Means Focusing

To focus on networking means interacting with the right people, identifying your own strengths and capabilities, and finding ways to increase your capacity. Know your own potential: if you're a power-seller, use that fact and share knowledge, tips, and tools with junior salespeople. If you're a psychology expert, focus on compiling your research into a series of educational lectures for graduate students. If you're a new fashion designer, focus on meeting significant players and give them assistance in planning magical, luxurious shows: they'll help you with your own launch when the time is right.

When you focus very strongly on your own objective, you'll find other people who "fit" your mission and can help you accomplish it. These people demonstrate the "right stuff" to fit your circle of associates: but you won't find them unless you talk your own talk *and* walk your own walk.

By demonstrating your integrity, doing a stellar job, and using your skills to benefit your company, you will meet more and more people who can help you in your mission. Prioritize personal and company improvements, and you'll attract friends who focus on their own business and perform at the top of their own game. Your internet presence gives you multiple options to focus on your target market: use it wisely.

Your current circle of associates earns approximately the same amount of net income that you do. If you're looking to increase your profits, expand your abilities, or perform at a higher level, you'll want to find people who are engaging and interacting with their companies or clients at a level slightly higher than your current status.

As an example of prioritizing, focusing, and being very clear about "finding the right people," I want to share my own experience finding clients. In my first year of business, my partner and I were willing to take on "anyone" for "any kind" of web project. This almost guaranteed that we found people wanting major web work for minimal pay! As time passed, we became much more selective and thoughtful about the types of projects we would agree to take on, and as a result we became much more efficient, provided more value to to our clients, became more cost-effective, and earned more per project. By focusing on the best, we attracted the best. You can do the same.

Tip 28
Be Personable:
Meet People Online and Offline

Many smart women know how to succeed academically or do a great job in the office, but how many realize that most of their professional lives are determined by "who they know?" Who do you know? Who do you work with? Is "who will help us?" your first question when you tackle a new project or initiative? The "who" question, probably the most important question, will be the first to pop into your mind when you need to find contacts that help you with your current task at hand. For example, if a catering company commits to landing five new clients, all in the $15k - $20k range per event, which questions might they ask?

The question of **WHY?** Probably not a great starting question. If you've committed, then start "dialing for dollars" to find *who* will help you get your project rolling.

The question of **HOW?** True leaders find others to help them do the mechanics of the work. If you don't know how to do a project, find someone who does know: this relates from line staff all the way up to C-level executives.

The question of **WHEN?** Your timeline totally depends on the involved parties. With lackluster people on your team, expect lackluster results. With stars on your team, start rolling immediately and arrive at your destination more smoothly. Your answer to the "who" question makes a big difference.

The question of **WHAT?** Who you know determines the answer to this question. Find a networking princess, an early adopter, a well-connected person, or someone more experienced to give you tips and advice on solutions. Find information through people who best know the type of project you're planning to accomplish.

WHO will help us? (Hint! This is the best question to ask first.) When you're looking for the best question to ask when starting a new project, begin with "Who will help us?"

The network you have established will determine your success. You will call upon other friends, associates, and coworkers to help you achieve your goals. If you're the caterer looking for five new $20k clients, you'll call around for event planners and decision makers for gala company dinners, product launches, and employee-wide events for Fortune 100 companies. You'll call your corporate events contacts; you'll call companies with upcoming anniversaries or founder events and connections who will know contacts at targeted companies. Ask "who may help us?", and watch your personal and professional success flourish.

When you don't yet have a stuffed Rolodex, or your contact database only numbers in the dozens, think about ways to meet other people. The key to meeting others lies in making your personal connection helpful to them.

What skills or tools do you offer that benefit others? Perhaps you have connections in a particular industry, or you have some articles on your field of expertise that you're willing to share, or you may do some volunteer work or consulting to a nonprofit or community group. Grow your circle of trusted contacts by finding ways to help others.

When you are meeting with others at an event or seminar, I recommend you organize your time and focus on meeting with a few new people for longer stretches of time instead of attempting to hand your card to everyone in the room. It is impossible to establish a meaningful connection with more than fifteen people at a two-hour event, so focus on table mates or people in your corner of the room. Consider following up directly or within a few days following the event, with a re-introduction and answers to any questions, referrals, or resource tips you've discussed. Some businesswomen add a picture of themselves to their outgoing mail signature to facilitate recognition.

It's easy to develop conversation topics: crystallize a 20-second "elevator pitch" about what your company offers to succinctly and clearly explain your unique approach. When asking others about their business, include questions about their specific functions, their interests, trends in their field, or any ideas they have on the types of clients they seek: you'll find mutually beneficial ways to help each other when you know each other and start the process of trusting each other.

Here's an example of a 20-second pitch, for a new jewelry business. Switch out adjectives or rework as necessary:

"My name is Luisa, and my business (INSERT NAME OF BUSINESS) matches beautiful jewelry to beautiful women. The perfect piece of jewelry adds style/flair/pizazz/a finishing touch to any working woman's wardrobe, and my customized/unique/gracious designs will make your business associates, wives, mothers, and daughters feel beautiful, confident, and polished. Going from work to play, these versatile pieces make every woman feel beautiful: choose a piece as a gift for a wedding, anniversary, birthday, or special event. Some samples are here [remember to wear samples!], and this month we're having a seasonal special of _____. I'm also looking for connections to wedding planners for beautiful bridal gifts for their customers."

Finally, I do believe in the creed from my Brownie days: a stranger is a friend you just don't know yet. Keep a positive attitude at new events. Your ability to understand other people translates very directly into your ability to be a resource to other people. When you're in business, your ability to understand other people's needs with great clarity directly translates into you being a resource person or a source of referrals to customers. Increase your skills in listening and understanding, and you will gain great advantages in your business life.

Tip 29
Use Social Networking: An Overview

Why bother with social networking? With the incredible amounts of visual and audio information out there, you have little time to make an impact. Many of us receive thousands of advertising messages a day. So, in response, some resort to personal recommendations from friends, family, and associates. If referrals are the lifeblood of any organization, and reputation-based word of mouth is one of the most trusted and highest-converting methods of making a sale, then your ability to get your message out to "people who make a difference" will enhance your net profit, guaranteed.

The curve of information is steadily and quickly moving towards social networking sites such as YouTube, Facebook, and Wikipedia. User-generated content, such as blogs, podcasts, images, and videos, are also rising quickly in importance. A corporate PR blog may be overshadowed by a blogger's inside scoop. A homemade YouTube video may be more popular than a carefully controlled corporate message. Furthermore, with so many people who have an ability to research your company, your motivation, and your personal "dirt," any kind of duplicity or lack of integrity will most definitely be uncovered. Witness the "fake" Walmart blog (created by a web company purporting to be RV-ers) and the fake Sony PlayStation3 YouTube video log, both of which were exposed easily by the blogging community.

People most naturally connect with like-minded people. If you're reaching your client community online, you are already two or three steps ahead of anyone who is attempting to broadcast to a generalized audience with a bland, unfocused message. Current trends in advertising for newspapers, television, and radio point to the demise of these broad-scale efforts and the rise of a more strategic approach to finding clients through targeted messaging with niche communities.

When you actively engage your potential customers and your existing clients by offering questions, feedback, and an ability to contribute to your work (like open source user contributions or through public customer comment cards), you're leveling the playing field for everyone. You are also adding value to your users, and you're responding to your market. When you develop products and services directly in response to a strongly stated need from your clientele, you support your customers, and you help convert their ideas into realtime solutions.

For women, the internet offers a level playing field where your words, ideas, art, music, or ability to communicate are more important than your appearance, gender, relationship status, nationality, religion, or cultural heritage. When you keep "on message" with what you represent, your customers will naturally gravitate to you because you're one of their "tribe."

I believe that social networking is the future of the Internet. When you share your knowledge of diapering techniques or soy candles or best places to visit in Italy or hardwood floors, you're providing an educated opinion that helps someone else make up their mind about that topic. When you share your knowledge freely (such as on a blog or podcast), you increase your ability to spread your knowledge, you connect with people interested in your topics, and you build a community of people who care about common goals.

On the web today, many expect knowledge to be free, so your added value comes from your expertise in your particular field. Share your basic knowledge but sell your skills as a high-level consultant, strategist, or industry authority. Some great examples include public relations tips blogs run by professionals who offer free tips as well as paid consultations, home mortgage analysis websites with calculators and resource tools and an option to contact the mortgage company, or baby product reviews with customer comments, run by a store owner who also sells the products.

As an aside, please note that if you are a company employee with specific knowledge of a product or service and you are not an official company press representative, you walk a fine line between sharing ongoing developments and disclosing company trade secrets. In my opinion, you must always represent yourself as a single individual who shares your own opinions. Add a disclaimer to your statements to clarify your positions.

My belief is that the rise of user-generated content and online communities will foster an era of cross-cultural understanding, a feeling, especially among younger people, of being part of a global village, and a sense of personal responsibility with an eye to a larger, holistic world view.

Two of my more well-used social networking sites are LinkedIn and Facebook. While very different in terms of purpose, levels of formality, layout, and user tools, both of these sites focus around person-to-person interaction and "six degrees of separation." Facebook is like a clubhouse. LinkedIn is like a professional networking seminar.

LinkedIn http://www.linkedin.com

This service focuses on professional and career-minded networking. Post your past and current jobs, education, and work associates. Your profile displays professional achievements, accomplishments, and your areas of expertise. When you connect with associates (from past jobs), your network grows. You may request introductions to those in your circle and your associates' circles.

As a special note, the "Recommendation" feature on LinkedIn helps provide outside validation and messages of praise for your work: these may help smooth the way to your next transaction. I've used my LinkedIn network to receive testimonials, update my professional profile, and connect with other women in business. The "Question and Answers" section in LinkedIn offers up-to-the-minute and in-depth answers to work-related topics.

Facebook http://www.facebook.com

With large numbers of Gen-X and Millennial users, this free service functions like your "clubhouse" for you and your friends. It's informal and focuses on a profile where you list your "wall" of interests and activities. You also may write on your friends' "walls." Choose from thousands of add-on applications to personalize your profile, including book reviews, Netflix feeds, music downloads, world map quizzes, and music. While I primarily use this tool to meet friends online and to share information in an informal way, I've also used Facebook to find and connect with friends from as far back as elementary school.

One of the barriers to using these sites is that they're not effective if you are the only person in your network to use them. When you log on, use the "Friend Finder" or "Search New Contacts" function to search for existing connections in your Gmail or Yahoo or Hotmail account. Alternatively, invite trusted associates to join your networks. I do recommend you "claim your name" so no one else may purport to be you, especially if you are building up your personal brand recognition in your field.

The following are more ideas on integrating social networking tools into your professional brand.

YouTube http://www.youtube.com

This viral video site offers social networking for people uploading pre-made videos. Videos may be tagged, categorized, and shared. If you upload a movie, it must be your own work, not someone else's copyrighted material.

One of the best video promotions I've seen is called "Will it Blend?" by Blendtec: a hilarious and unexpected series of snippets with a white-coated technician testing the Blendtec blender against a variety of items (action figure, lighters, SPAM, iPhone, tiki torch, scissors), all with a "Do not try this at home" disclaimer. You'll remember the videos because they're amusing and vivid. Filipina-American comedienne Christine of "Happy Slip" developed a base of followers on YouTube before selling DVDs of her hilarious skits directly to her fans. If your business lends itself to demonstration, start posting to YouTube, Google Video, or Yahoo! Video. Use a digital video camera, a cell phone, or even a collection of static images. You may upload videos tagged with links and specific keywords.

Meetup http://www.meetup.com

Meetup's easy-to-use organizing tools allow you to find other people with similar interests in person, in your location. The site targets niche markets, from French language to scrapbooking to goth to classical music. If your business fits a specific industry, consider visiting a Meetup event to find like-minded partners, associates, or customers. The site offers a search by keyword, zip code, country, or city. Register to signal your intent to participate in a group, or just show up at a scheduled event. If you enjoy the gathering, register for upcoming meeting notifications.

MySpace http://www.myspace.com

One of the first sites to have in-depth profile pages, this site offers music clips, video displays, a list of friends, and a blog update page. Primarily for the younger audience, the site focuses heavily on music, films, and entertainment. If you're in these industries, claim your band or group name. Users personalize their own pages, but a drawback of the coding for this site includes the ability for spammers and phishers to insert malicious code into their profiles, which then impact your machine or your privacy if you visit those pages accidentally. I highly recommend this site for entertainment related businesses.

Flickr http://www.flickr.com

Flickr, the Yahoo!-based photo-sharing site, offers storage for photos. If your business thrives on before-and-after photos of your work in action or if you best market your products through visual media, a Flickr account helps you share your skills. Organize your Flickr photos into sets, "tag" them with keywords, and specify photo viewing permissions. You may upload photos directly from your desktop or even post photos by e-mail. Flickr would not be appropriate for your business if your images are confidential or if they contain material that owners/subjects would prefer to keep private.

Twitter http://www.twitter.com

With this application, send out "tweets" via the twitter website or your mobile phone, and update people who are "following" you. The most striking example I have recently used this site for is keeping abreast of developments during the San Diego wildfires in October 2007. My family was evacuated, and different internet news feeds were slowed down by intense website traffic. One station switched to Twitter to send out up-to-the-minute updates. When you use Twitter in conjunction with your blog, you have a powerful informational tool that you may update by phone or computer from anywhere in the world.

Digg http://www.digg.com

Digg, a user community, offers "tagging" for news or links with notable content. Use this site to receive insight into the overall status of a site by displaying how many "diggs" a link receives. You may also search on a specific keyword to see what's "Digg-worthy" in the web and blogosphere for your industry, field, specialty, or name.

StumbleUpon http://www.stumbleupon.com

This installable toolbar allows users to find sites, videos, and photos that other people have deemed worthy to visit. StumbleUpon feeds you potential links based on your past favorite links. If you've tagged a website that you like, the toolbar sends you even more targeted links.

Del.icio.us http://www.del.icio.us

This social bookmarking site uses a toolbar or your browser to save your bookmarks, tag them, and find them again. Post a link to your bookmarks list and access it at any time from any other web browser. You may also provide a "feed" of your tagged links to your own web pages (I offer a list of del.icio.us links tagged "business" on my own sites). The del.icio.us website offers an easy way to keep bookmarks in one place online, instead of spread out onto multiple machines.

Wikipedia http://www.wikipedia.org

Wikipedia, the online encyclopedia, offers a member-editable list of notable people, places, things, and ideas. While not exhaustive, the site offers multiple language options and many types of subjects. You might want to contribute to a wiki on a particular subject and keep it updated if you have your own published research on a topic or field.

New technology arrives every day, so keep abreast by visiting Wired.com or TechCrunch.com if these types of tools interest you. Some additional ways to use social networking sites include organizing documents or people into one focused group, uploading files to one particular listserv, offering teleconference, phone, internet, e-mail, text, or chat-based solutions to your customers, maintaining a group calendar or blog, or finding ways to organize your to-do lists and documents via a web-based location such as Google Groups or Basecamp.

Internal "wikis" also provide a way to share information and updates between like-minded people or those on a group or team. Web software that fosters group interaction, such as Google Docs or applications on Facebook or LinkedIn, will contribute to your intent when you are building your social network. In many cases, being connected to at least 150 people yields potential connections to over a million others. Social networking will help you spread the word about your own projects and increase the quality and quantity of your "reach."

As a final note, committing to opening an account on some of these social networking sites does require from you a certain amount of time to keep your information current. However, time spent by you is also time spent by potential customers on these sites! For example, Facebook founder Mark Zuckerberg estimates that 50% of registered users return to their Facebook profile every day. He also posted that Facebook is the sixth most trafficked site on the internet and drives more photo postings and event invitations than any other site in the United States.

While you're shaping your internet strategy for the next five years, consider using social networking sites as your base for reaching targeted, niche customers in your specific field of interest. Get acquainted with the currently available sites.

Tip 30
Show, Don't Tell: Add a Demonstration

If you have a product or service that benefits from a "show-and-tell" approach, consider creating a demonstration section on your homepage, or create a series of video posts explaining different aspects of your business. Human beings respond very well to moving images, especially videos with people, animals, or babies, sound effects, or three-dimensional objects.

If your product or service demands a more in-depth review that would benefit from the highly visual nature of film, tell your story using your image and voice. Some samples to think about include: hosting a job site or office walk-through, demonstrating your process in a step-by-step manner, including testimonials from other customers, animating an item and rotating it in multiple dimension, or doing video introductions to key people on your staff.

Videos do not need to be complex. A 15-second, 30-second, or one minute introduction to your company may suffice. Place demonstration videos or company-focused videos on your website, with credits and links, as needed. You may host your videos on your site in a variety of formats (Quicktime, Flash, or Real Media). Also consider publishing your videos to free services like YouTube, Google, Yahoo! or Facebook for added exposure.

A useful addition to your team will be a digital videographer, digital storyteller, film or production crew, or someone who may compile your still images, text, and/or music into a final video that helps sell your work. Find referrals through your local community college, your network, or through other reputable sources.

Checklist for delivering video on your website:
☐ Quick load time for your video
☐ Pictures of you, your staff, your work site, or your products within the video
☐ Music, voice, or sound effects as desired
☐ Call to action: your contact information embedded in the video
☐ Contact information is updated and correct
☐ Provide alternate methods of delivery for viewers without the appropriate software
☐ Keep it short and sweet
☐ Break larger videos into smaller "chunks"
☐ Provide trailers, quick demonstrations, or product highlights

- [ ] If needed, offer a link from a "teaser" version to a longer version
- [ ] Add captioning or text equivalents to your videos as desired
- [ ] Publish videos through multiple channels, starting with your website and moving to social networking sites or industry sites.
- [ ] Videos may be hosted on your own site or on YouTube, Google, Yahoo! Video, or any video-sharing site
- [ ] Check for appropriate tags and descriptions on your videos
- [ ] Check that your video is appropriate and relevant to other types of videos hosted on a shared service
- [ ] If e-mailing, always share a link to the video on a web page: do NOT embed a large video file into your outgoing e-mail
- [ ] Add a link to your new video in your e-newsletter, your e-mail signature, or in your "what's new" section

Tip 31
Comment Thoughtfully on Other Sites

A suggestion for expanding your network of interested clients online is to use your person-to-person skills to visit, comment on, and contribute to websites that you enjoy reading.

For example, when you participate in a blog community, you provide thoughtful commentary and possible additions or updates to the author's blog posts. Refrain from posting "drive-by comments." For a comment to be useful, you actually must take the time to understand the blog author's platform, to provide helpful comments, suggestion, or criticism, to subscribe to their feed, or to otherwise engage with the author/s. Many bloggers become your trusted business associates because of the types of comments you post and the quality of your responses to the situations they blog about.

There are a number of web visitors who get most of their news through news readers, through pre-set alerts on certain subject keywords, or through aggregators. Being specific in every item that you post on and always including comments, keywords, or search engine phrases that match your business will help interested parties "find" you.

When posting comments, include a link to your own website, and remember that your comments may be picked up by the search engines. For consistency, while you are networking via comment boards or comments on postings, do exercise prudence.

As a note, if you find errors, omissions, typos, or incorrect information on a website, do bring that information to the web contact or the blog owner: they will be able to correct their errors and provide even more useful, professional information.

Finally, when you are a part of a blogroll or a community of people who link to each other, keep the conversation going and periodically "tag" each other with "memes" that are easy ways to personalize the subject matter or provide even more information. You'll find many others who share your interests: connect with them via your website, and reap the benefits of having friends and associates all over the world.

Tip 32
Are you Legitimate? Add Testimonials

Being Filipino means my family knows how to eat well. While I was growing up, my mom (and grandmothers) always told me to have Chinese food only at a restaurant where there are lots of other people in line. Tip: If you see Chinese people eating at a Chinese restaurant, the food is probably delicious. Have you ever joined a line for a restaurant because there were other people in line? Have you ever chosen a particular dentist, doctor, pediatrician, or any kind of specialist based on your friend's or family member's recommendation? People "love" to go with other people's recommendations.

It doesn't matter what you're selling—it may be cell phone service, tires, computers, organic fruit snacks, lumber, or handicrafts. Your customers, if they spread the word about you, will be your biggest salespeople because people **love** to go with recommendations.

The power of testimonials is huge. A transaction will close much more quickly when you have a third party vouching for your work. Testimonials sell your services, and referrals from other satisfied clients help you close a sale much more quickly. To assist with your sales, put your testimonials on your website. Other options include adding a testimonial to your e-mail signature, adding a "past clients" page on your blog, and adding specific, targeted quotations from real people who you've helped, along with samples of how you've solved their problem or contributed to their happiness. Your testimonials help cautious buyers decide if you're a good fit for them.

When creating your testimonial list, choose quality over quantity. Ask some favorite clients to give you feedback, and add their quotes to your service offerings. Make sure these recommendations identify what truly sets your brand apart.

Examples of effective testimonials include:

1) **Visual Artists, Photographers, Designers**
Keep an album of finished projects, even from your early days, that you may have on hand for a potential client. This method works particularly well for photographers or artists: you'll be expected to bring along samples of your work to show that you're effective and competent and

that your style matches what your client seeks.

2) People Who Deal with Personal Issues

Most recommendations for therapists, counselors, coaches, and body-related specialists such as doulas, acupuncturists, and massage therapists, will come from current clients. If you are building up your business, consider doing reduced-price work for friends and associates in order to create a list of satisfied clients. Use their testimonials and encourage them to refer a friend. As you build a larger base of clients, your referrals will increase exponentially. My midwife has been operating this way for over 20 years.

3) Physical Exhibits of Your Work

Artists, contractors, painters, roofers, interior decorators, organizers, architects, and other consultants who work in the physical dimension will want to take "before" and "after" pictures. You'll also want to provide physical representations of your work, like scale models, plans, and/or drawings. Add these items to your website. In addition, provide local references: for example, if you've recently re-roofed a house, tell your next client the address of that house so they may drive by and review your work with their own eyes.

When you organize your testimonials into a photo gallery, list of reviews, montage, downloadable resources section, case studies section, or simply some well-placed quotations, you show potential customers how you've solved similar issues to the ones they're currently facing. From your customers' point of view, they are faced with a bewildering array of options: your ability to identify similar situations and your targeted response will give them an easy choice by going with you and your solution.

Checklist for using testimonials:
- [ ] Collect quotes from satisfied clients
- [ ] Specify the details of a challenge and your proposed solution
- [ ] Explain what you were able to accomplish for your customer
- [ ] Choose quality testimonials over quantity
- [ ] Add samples, photos, or downloads to show your solution
- [ ] Specify what sets you apart
- [ ] What makes your company unique?
- [ ] What benefits does your company provide?
- [ ] Why do customers choose you over and above others?

Tip 33
Photo Gallery: Provide Samples of your Work

A well-placed photo gallery does wonders to demonstrate your work. Collect images and videos of your work: simple digital camera pics or even scans of hard copies will be effective. Take some time to edit your display collection into specific categories, such as color, industry, or topical area. Choose the best samples, and display them proudly.

Place your images in a photo gallery section with the ability for the user to click-through to larger versions, if available. You may use your web statistics to review which galleries web visitors navigate to most often: place those popular galleries at a higher level or highlight them on your homepage.

If your company allows it or it fits your mission, also consider adding an "upload your own" section for website visitors. These may be informal sections such as "viewer suggestions" or "post a solution" to solicit your website visitors' creative process. You'll want a way to easily delete potentially negative images if you offer a public section like this.

Before and after photos tend to be very popular with your web visitors. Professional organizers, interior decorators, and landscapers use this function to very good effect on their websites. Also consider product demonstrations, wrap-around views, schematics, randomized images, or rotating views to enhance your gallery.

Some tools to help organize your photos include Flickr, Smugmug, or Ofoto. If you'd like to put your photos onto merchandise (mugs, cards, t-shirts, baseball caps, etc.), consider uploading your images to Zazzle or Cafepress. All of these provide easy ways to display your images, and all allow you to copy-and-paste codes that link these products to your website.

As a final note, always make sure that any photos are easy for your web visitor to review: strive to "optimize" your photos by reducing the size and the dots per inch so they load into a web browser efficiently and easily.

Checklist for photo galleries:
☐ Photo Gallery includes Title of Photo, Description, and/or Photographer Credit

- [ ] Ask for permission from photographers and/or subjects
- [ ] Images are no more than 800 pixels wide or 800 pixels high
- [ ] Try saving images at a lower resolution for website delivery
- [ ] If you are concerned about reproduction of your own images, add a watermark or other identifying mark to your photos
- [ ] For additional copyright management, display your photos at a low resolution or smaller size
- [ ] Choose photo-sharing software or online tools that do not require registration for visitors to view your work
- [ ] Place links to your photo gallery throughout your site
- [ ] Sprinkle randomized photos on your web pages
- [ ] Photos reflect your organization, clientele, and/or staff

Tip 34
Share your Values: Report on your Vision

A well-highlighted mission, vision, and values statement does wonders to clarify what type of company you represent, what you are accomplishing, how you do business, and what values your business embodies.

Consider adding a "Social Responsibility Report Card," a goals statement, or a list of your company values in a prominent place on your website. When you highlight your company's vision, visitors understand what you find important and how your business is operated: this helps target your clients even more.

For example, if you have received green certification for your business, you have a LEED-rated facility, you are part of the Better Business Bureau, or you've been awarded a designation, recognition, or special certificate for your industry, add that logo, link, or explanation to your website footer or in a special section.

When you highlight the company values statement, you also add additional page content that connects your website to those keywords, which further increases your page relevance for those specific references.

Checklist of ideas for statements:
- [ ] Mission Statement
- [ ] Vision Statement
- [ ] Our Values
- [ ] Our Goals
- [ ] What We Believe
- [ ] Our Principles
- [ ] What We Stand For
- [ ] Why We're in Business
- [ ] What You Can Expect
- [ ] Customer Satisfaction Policy
- [ ] Company Report Card
- [ ] Environmental Sustainability

Summary to Keep in Mind: Target your Clients

Your base of targeted clients forms your most important asset, especially when they adore your company, have given you permission to market to them, and buy all your products and services. To find these "right" people, you'll need to focus on the specific type of clientele you want to serve. Focusing on an ideal target client gives you the ability to find that client with more ease.

To find your targeted clients, you'll meet potential referrals and associates both on the web and in person, like at networking meals, industry events, or conferences. Use your natural interests, and practice being personable to meet others.

Social networking through a variety of web-based tools, such as LinkedIn and Facebook, may also help when you're expanding your network. Combine online activities with offline activities, such as attending a Meetup gathering in your specific field: in this way you establish person-to-person connections while you expand your contact list.

When you demonstrate rather than explain, you accomplish more: use a video to increase your reach and "touch" people who respond well to moving images and sounds. A video may be a simple collection of images and text, or it may be a full 5-minute commercial that highlights your message: choose something to fit your budget and expand your coverage as much as possible.

By participating in other influential individuals' endeavors, you'll support others and expand your target audience through sharing. I encourage you to comment thoughtfully on other associates' blogs or to contribute to relevant bulletin boards and online communities. Each of your comments may be picked up by search engines, so use that opportunity to expand your web recognition and "meet" others in your market.

Rework your website to add testimonials or positive comments from others who admire and support your own work. When your customers sell your services and products, you enhance your own marketing techniques. Be aware that bad press from a few influential bloggers impacts you tremendously, too, so stay as genuine, transparent, and honest as possible.

If you offer a highly visual aspect to your work, consider adding photos or other samples to your gallery. Before and after treatments do a great job of selling your abilities, as do 360-degree walkthroughs, product demonstrations, or other innovative ways to demonstrate your company's expertise.

Finally, keep your values in the forefront of your mind, and keep them posted in a prominent website section. Your visitors will learn more about what drives your company, and your search rankings will include these value and vision keywords whenever someone performs a search on you or your company, business, or project.

Chapter 5:
Focus on Usability

- If They Can't Use It, They Won't Use It
- 35. Browser Basics: Elements of your Layout
- 36. The Queen of Links: Check for Error Pages
- 37. Standards: Move to a CSS Version
- 38. The Extras: Audio, Video, and Flash
- 39. Share How it Works: Add a Checklist
- 40. Help Your Visitors: Use Easy Navigation
- 41. Whip Out the Credit Card: Encourage Online Payments
- 42. A Call to Action: Offer it on Every Page
- Summary to Keep in Mind: Focus on Usability

If They Can't Use It, They Won't Use It

You want visitors to use your website effectively, and you want your message to go directly to your target users with minimal "noise" and distractions.

Jakob Nielsen of Useit.com has published years of research where he and his team observe users interacting with websites. Too many users click away in frustration because they cannot find the price of a product, a photo doesn't load, information doesn't make sense within the layout, or the user just doesn't find the information they need. In my experience, users also click away from your website if the site doesn't "look right," if it hasn't been updated, or if there's no "About Us" page.

Make your website as readable and viewable as possible by reducing clutter and keeping the layout simple, checking broken pages, moving to a CSS (Cascading Style Sheets) version of your site, and monitoring interactive elements to make sure they work in different browsers and platforms.

When planning the site's design, work with your web developer to create a detailed site map that lays out the different pages and priorities of each piece of web content. Navigation level pages display on every page, while sub-navigation or stand-alone pages display depending on the section.

In my experience, clarity of thinking in the very beginning of the web design process translates to a better layout for the site, which results in an easier and more positive experience for your web user. Make your site as easy to use as possible. Your visitors will thank you.

When you put yourself in your web visitors' seat, you'll be able to look at your website with the eyes of a "newbie." Do you find what you're looking for? Does the site feel legitimate? Would you trust the company or person behind this website? Can you learn more about the company mission, services, products, or background of the chief officers? Would you want to buy from this company?

If you can truthfully answer "YES" to those questions, you're probably on the right track to using your website to create an honest representation of your business.

Tip 35
Browser Basics: Elements of your Layout

Maintain your site's consistency from page to page, and your web visitor will have an easier time navigating through the layout. The four main components of any site break down into the following:

> a) a top bar section which includes the logo, the motto, images, or another interesting visual "hook"

> b) the content of the page, with the block of text that is the main focus of that page

> c) the footer of the page, with legal notices, policies and disclaimers, a site map, copyright notices, or other important information

> d) optional: sidebars on the left and/or right side of the page, with additional information relevant to that section or page

When you deliberately place items in "hot spots" that users always look at, such as the top center of the page, the top left and side left, and the bottom of the page, you have better control over how visitors click through your site. Most web developers recommend putting your "About Us" and "Products" or "Services" pages in these sections.

If your website is a business or corporate site, strive to keep it as free of surprises as possible. If your website is not entertainment, media, or gaming-based, keep those four basic components on every page for consistency and to build your web users' confidence in you, your website, and your message. If your website is an entertainment, media, or gaming-based site, you have some more flexibility, and you may choose to work with a more engaging layout, more multimedia, a less rigid design, and more daring content.

Whatever the circumstance, make sure to accurately reflect your company's products, services, and potential user base within your website's "look-and-feel." Keep your target clients close to you, and they'll feel like your home on the web is their home, too.

Tip 36
The Queen of Links: Check for Error Pages

Be vigilant about broken links, which continue to plague many sites. Link checking includes checking all links within your navigation and text. An automatic tool you may use is Xenu's Link Sleuth (TM)

http://home.snafu.de/tilman/xenulink.html

Or, submit your site to Google Webmasters and their automatic spider will find any 404 (Page Not Found) errors. If you're using a database-driven site like Wordpress, Joomla, Drupal or some other content management system (CMS), your site has slightly less chance of displaying broken links because each page is generated specifically from the database. You may always check your web statistics to see if there are any 404 errors (file not found) in your visitor records.

It is possible to specify how you want your "missing" page to display. Some people redirect any missing pages directly to the homepage. Alternatively, you might have a "missing" page that includes helpful additional tips or a list of the most recently viewed links within the site. Ask your web developer or your hosting company how they handle 404 errors. Give them guidelines on how you want broken pages to still behave like a part of your website so your end user may find their target destination.

Checklist for 404 error pages:
☐ Develop a custom "Missing"/404 Error page
☐ Redirect to other relevant pages if a page is missing
☐ Display links to highly relevant items
☐ Keep your visitor on your website, even if a link is broken!
☐ Check website records to see what pages are "Missing"/404 and fix these pages

Tip 37
Standards: Move to a CSS Version

The World Wide Web Consortium (W3C) develops protocols and guidelines to ensure the long-term growth for the web: http://www.w3c.org. The W3C takes charge of developing standards for easier web access, especially to comply with different methods of web browsing (such as mobile phones or small screens). Additional standards include offering ways for disabled users to still be able to review your page content.

Within the web development community there has been a switchover towards separating form from content, and one standard you may hear about is the issue of Cascading Style Sheets (CSS) to control content delivery.

A knowledgeable web developer will know how to best integrate CSS into your website. Typically things like paragraph styles, heading styles, and images may be updated site-wide by using CSS standards. Many (if not most) legacy sites rely on <font> tags, table-based layout (using rows and columns to make a page appear a certain way), and other non-CSS functions. However, when you upgrade, redesign, or start off with a new site, a

CSS-based layout may help your web developer and designer create a comprehensive look-and-feel for the whole website.

The debate about standards compliance has been going on for many years now, but, in general, clean, easy-to-understand code will rely on many "div" tags, which your web developer will help you integrate into your site. "Divs" allow you to organize the content on a webpage into different "layers" that may be grouped and modified according to your needs. When properly set up, they can make changing the look and feel of the content a more efficient process. This will save you time and money in the long run at no additional up front charge.

While a site may not be standards-specific and will still render fine within a browser, I do recommend you move towards "standards compliancy" and "table-less layouts" for your future web development efforts.

Tip 38
The Extras: Audio, Video, and Flash

Many websites use audio, video, and Flash elements to enhance the display or to provide more interactive content. Sample files or tools you'll hear about include Flash, Ajax, Quicktime, Realplayer, or other types of files.

My rule of thumb for additional items such as these is to consider your target market and understand if users would benefit from these extra items.

Would a two-minute movie demonstrate your process better than pages upon pages of technical content? Would a "how-to" video save time and answer questions? Would a friendly introductory message from you help engage or inform your customer? If so, invest in the time to create a high-quality explanatory video and deliver that video in a prominent place on your website. However, if your target users do not desire or need additional graphics or sound, you may end up distracting them with too many "bells and whistles" on your website, so choose wisely.

If you are a sole proprietor or you would like to show samples of your process or product in action, I do recommend adding a montage or film clip with sound or interactive elements to display your work. Short demonstrations such as procedures, slideshows, or technically specific processes also benefit from video delivery.

Typical uses of web video include product demonstrations, tutorials or how-to sample videos, snippets of your work, interviews, on-site visits, programming relevant to your company, or even news clips that mention your product and services. Typical places where video or audio may be delivered include Google, YouTube, Yahoo!, Vimeo, and other third-party services, as well as video or audio in MP3 format or Quicktime placed directly on your website.

Speak with your web developer, and decide on the best way to deliver your message.

Tip 39
Share How it Works: Add a Checklist

In my experience, adding a checklist, a step-by-step list, or a page that explains your business procedure "flow" helps your customers understand what to expect when they work with you. For example, a real estate agent may want to add a list of the general milestones within the process of buying or selling a house. Specifying goals, key markers, stopping points, or "what to look for" at any of those milestones may also help the web visitor understand your process.

You want to make it as easy as possible for a potential customer to work with you, and adding a checklist may help ease the burden of explaining your process over the phone.

Some web visitors will prefer to read your checklist, some will prefer an audio version, some will prefer a visual representation, and others might prefer a movie or short video demonstration.

Accommodate your web visitors as much as possible by displaying your process in multiple formats. Once your customers know what to expect, you make it far easier for them to say "yes" to what you're offering online.

When you offer a "Preview" section, or a "Try Before You Buy" feature, you also encourage your customer to become familiar with your website products or services before committing to buying from you. Offer basic or "light" versions to give your customer a chance to decide.

For example, we offer sample product demonstrations and an opportunity to view screenshots of our "back-end control panel." Do you have some information you may share about your company that will help your customer make an informed decision? Consider the local grocery store, where you often may find sample-size portions or freebies/giveaways for new products. These methods work to generate interest and "buzz" about the new drink or snack product: customers love to have a "taste" of what you're selling, so come up with a creative way to offer samples of your wares.

Tip 40
Help Your Visitors:
Use Easy Navigation

When you look at a printed road map, you see larger font sizes for major cities, and you see heavier lines for important freeways and roads. When you decide on your website navigation, use larger text and bolded or highlighted graphical elements to point out your important page content. Keep your navigation and sub-navigation consistent across all your pages to provide your visitors with a satisfying, easy-to-use experience.

If your site only offers sub-navigation on separate content pages, you may be due for a redesign. An example would be an "About Us" page where a visitor may find sub-navigation links to Mission, Vision, Values, History, Board, and Staff. In an ideal situation, you make those sub-navigation links available on every page within the site, not just on the About Us page.

A redesign with drop-down menus gives your users access to every part of the site and helps them understand their current position on the site and how that page relates to the other pages.

A "breadcrumb" feature may also be helpful when you have multiple levels of subcategorization. Help your users understand your website by giving them an easy way to navigate throughout, within and between your different levels of page content. By helping them with basics like easy website navigation, you help visitors focus on your message, instead of focusing on how to navigate through your site.

Checklist for navigation:
- [ ] Is navigation clearly labeled?
- [ ] If desired, are there related pages available?
- [ ] Is there a "breadcrumb" or a way to understand where a current page lies in the overall hierarchy?
- [ ] Offer a site map for major navigational elements
- [ ] Is navigation consistent across all pages?
- [ ] If possible, show all sub-navigational elements from all pages so a user may review all available pages from any individual page

Tip 41
Whip Out the Credit Card: Encourage Online Payments

Startup businesses and companies need to focus on positive cash flow, and online payments may help with this process. Your web developer will give you a recommendation on how you may enhance your payment process. By adding credit card logos to your site, you signify your readiness to accept credit cards from your customers. This may shorten your sales cycle by a fair amount.

PayPal remains one of the most popular payment systems for consultants and startup businesses. By charging a 2.9% transaction fee and no monthly fees, PayPal gives you an easy and simple way to accept credit card payments, create and send invoices, and send packing slips. Authorize.net, Google Checkout, and e-Junkie.com also all provide different options for payment. Review your needs, and ask a resource person for additional options, or find more of my up-to-date reviews on asuccessfulwoman.com

Your banker or merchant account specialist will give you even more options for integrating a payment plan into your website. Being able to accept payments online gives you and your customer greater flexibility. Some samples of credit card payments include: one-time payments, shopping cart payments, annual dues collection, subscription fees, membership fees, deposit fees, recurring bill payments by month or by quarter, online invoicing and payments, donations online, and one-time payments.

To accept payments, you may offer clickable links on your website as well as online forms or downloadable PDF forms. Think about the most appropriate solution for your specific needs and budget.

Checklist for online payments:
☐ Display credit card icons (Visa, Mastercard, Discover, American Express)
☐ Explain your payment policies
☐ Display any privacy policies related to use of financial information
☐ Offer a returns or exchanges policy
☐ Shipping options and information included?
☐ Options for ship-to and bill-to, if needed?
☐ Explain how you keep information secure (you may copy this from your payment processor's site)

Tip 42
A Call to Action: Offer it on Every Page

When a visitor comes to your site because of the highly targeted content you're offering, make sure to retain your connection and contact with that visitor by offering a "call to action" on every page. This may include some or all of the following links to trigger additional action from your user:

- Contact us for more information
- Estimate your cost
- Sign up for our e-newsletter
- Send this e-mail to a friend
- Learn more about this process
- Download as a PDF
- Visit our resource library
- Buy now!
- Purchase this e-book
- Register for our course now

You want web visitors to continue interacting with your site, so offer opportunities to engage with a call to action. The "stickier" your site is, the more chances you have of earning your visitors' trust and turning them into happy customers.

Summary to Keep in Mind: Focus on Usability

You want everything about your website to foster customer confidence in your company, image, products and services. When your web visitors pay attention to your value proposition and understand your message, you have a greater chance of making a sale and building your base of clients. When your web visitors are distracted, frustrated, bored, or lost while visiting your site, you have a much higher barrier to encouraging a sale. Keep in mind that maintaining a consistent layout from page to page fosters supreme confidence in your website and encourages more clicking throughout the site.

Increase your website usability by checking for broken links through your error logs or through link checker tools, by using CSS when your web developer recommends it, by adding audio, video, and flash sparingly and only if these elements increase your visitors' understanding of your products and services, and by offering a checklist to help your visitors understand the process of working with your company.

One of the more important ways to increase your website usability is to display consistent navigation and sub-navigation. By offering a consistent display, you allow your users the option to orient themselves within your site and easily click to the next relevant section.

Online payment processing is a boon to small business owners, consultants, and e-sellers. PayPal and other tools give you many options to accept Visa, Mastercard, American Express, Discover, and e-checks. Ask around for best ways to process typical payments through your website: you'll help your customer, and you'll also shorten your wait time for revenue.

Finally, a great way to make sure your website works for you is to offer a call to action on each and every page. By engaging your web visitor, you offer multiple ways for them to become a part of your community of clients. Offer a free e-newsletter, a sign-up sheet or registration form, a calendar of your upcoming events, a way to pay online, or a "buy now" button. Choose the most relevant way to use your website to sell to your customers.

In a novel, a good writer uses a "hook" at the end of each chapter to encourage you to turn the page and keep reading. For your website pages, be smart and find the best call to action for each page to encourage web visitors to continue clicking. You'll build up more time with potential clients and increase your chances of making a sale. Good ways to do this include crafting your own personal "story," providing details about who you are, what you offer, and what customers may expect when choosing your company, and offering ways for customers to continue their conversation with you through a sign-up sheet or some other interaction.

In the next chapter, we'll look a bit closer at how best to understand our visitors and use that data to give them even more ways to buy services and products through our websites.

Chapter 6: Measuring Data

- How to Inform Your Decisions
- 43. The Welcome Mat: Understand Who's Dropping By
- 44. Build the Path: Improve User "Flow"
- 45. Keep 'em Coming: Make your site "Sticky"
- 46. Data Tells the Truth: Use Your Site Reports
- 47. For Community-Building: Expanding your Reach
- Summary to Keep in Mind: Measure Your Data

How to Inform Your Decisions

The cycle of web development isn't complete until you review your data and make edits and "tweaks" to your site based on the feedback and reporting you receive.

Your website statistics (we use Google Analytics) are your most trusted tools for understanding how web visitors go through your site content. These reports give you in-depth data, such as the keywords used to visit your site, the types of browsers and operating systems your visitors use, the pages they visit, the length of time they spend on your site, and their home countries.

With time and more data from your website visitors, you may then make changes to keywords, page length and complexity, the order of your navigational pages, and other page content elements to target your visitors even more. By combining the data from your site visitors with feedback from your customers or people on your e-newsletter list, you get a much better picture of what's working and what may be improved on your website. Acting on that data then increases your website's efficacy even more, leading to more qualified leads and even better sales.

Tip 43
The Welcome Mat: Understand Who's Dropping By

Your website statistics report gives you information about who's visiting your site, which you may use to improve user experience. Available data points include:

1) **The keywords your website visitors use**. These are the actual keywords a web visitor types into the search engine to lead them to your site. These keywords help you understand how visitors find your page content. They may also give you great ideas on how to extend your page content, based on what your visitors seek.

2) **The specific pages your guests visit.** You'll notice that certain pages of your site receive much more traffic than others. Navigate through these pages, and make sure that each one includes relevant, updated information as well as your call to action and a way for visitors to contact you.

3) **The time users spend on your site.** You want your site to be a destination where visitors

feel like they may "get to know you" and your company. By checking the length of time a visitor spends on your site, you get a good sense of the quality of your content and its value to your guests. In some reports, you may also see the "entry" pages that first attract visitors and the "exit" pages from where visitors leave your site.

Some additional markers I use to understand web users include the visit frequency per user, the pages per user, the number of unique visitors, the referring sites, and the visitor's country.

Frequency of visits per user. If you're developing an ongoing fan base, online community, or blog, you'll want visitors to return to your site on a regular basis. Compare the numbers of your first-time visitors to the incidence of repeat visitors to understand who returns to see your freshly updated content. With a high frequency of visits per user, you're establishing a committed clientele who like to drop in to your site daily, weekly, or monthly.

Pages per user. Depending on your model, you may want a highly targeted base of customers visiting multiple pages within your site, or you may want multitudes of visitors checking one or two pages and leaving. Through website reports, you'll see how many pages the average user visits, and you may make changes accordingly. For example, if you'd offer a 'Related Pages' section with links at the bottom of each page, you encourage your casual web visitor to click through to your suggested links and potentially spend more time on your website. Use that additional time to explain your process and earn even more trust.

Number of unique visitors. This statistic is most commonly used to understand the number of unique computers that are accessing your site within a particular time frame. We use this number more than the "hit count" because this tells you the actual individual people who visit your website. This number doesn't take into consideration the same person who accesses your website from different machines during the day (for example, one person visiting from a home computer, an iPhone, and a work computer counts as three separate users), but the number may help you in doing your website tracking analysis.

Referral sites. Your referral list will tell you how your traffic gets generated: for example, someone may click on a link to your website within their e-mail. Alternatively, you may be listed on another blogroll, or you may be linked on another website. The referral list gives you a sense of how much traffic is generated from search engine listings, how much traffic is referred to you, and how much traffic occurs from someone typing your URL directly into their browser.

Country of origin. Some reporting tools give you an understanding of the geographical location of your web visitor. This may be helpful for you if you're based in multiple locations or are targeting specific types of clients around the world. Use this statistic to understand the origins and the languages that visitors are using to find your site.

Your sense of "who's dropping by" your website will help you understand how to best structure and organize your information. If many people are visiting your "Frequently Asked Questions" section, you know to expand it and make that page even more informative. If many people are visiting a specific resource page, you will understand how they found it and what kind of information visitors need from you. Your statistics provide an ongoing way for you to refine your website presence.

Make sure to thank those other people who refer website traffic to you and by extension, help with business and community-building opportunities.

Tip 44
Build the Path: Improve User "Flow"

With more understanding of who's visiting your website and how they're using the site, you may then reassess the natural "flow" of your information.

For example, if people always seem to click on the photo gallery, then include more sample photos embedded into your homepage or at the bottom of your pages. If your web users always go to your calendar of events, highlight the next few events in your sidebar to make it easier to find. If your visitors use your blog as their main entry point, make sure to reference your desired contact or product pages from the blog articles.

The user "flow" through the site may also be improved by rearranging navigation. You'll find that some pages receive much more traffic than others. For whatever reason, these pages have the most targeted information for your web visitors, so link to them in a "most requested pages" section, or make sure those pages are well-highlighted in your navigation or homepage text.

Within your navigation, the items to the top left typically receive more visits than other items, so make sure those areas include your most important links like "About Us" or "How to Get Involved."

With more insight into how people use your website, you may enhance their experience and make their time spent with you even more enjoyable, informative, and mutually beneficial.

Tip 45
Keep 'em Coming: Make your site "Sticky"

One of the most popular sections on our membership sites are the "hotseat" questionnaires where visitors and members may learn a little more revealing information about a member who's volunteered to share. Similar to the "Bonus Features" section of a DVD, a behind-the-scenes approach may interest more visitors, so offer some informal sections to supplement your main informational pages.

Other popular sections within any website include photo galleries of any sort (these often constitute the most highly-visited pages on a site, second only to the homepage), a videos page, a "Highlight of the Month" page featuring something or someone of interest, a more in-depth "About Us" page with additional photos and stories, and an ongoing news and events or blog section with the latest highlights from your organization or company. You might also engage readers with a "Sneak Preview" page, a "From the Readers" page, an "Uploads" page for visitors to input their own information, or some other way to disseminate your information in a way that fosters conviviality and mutual sharing. Some news sites now offer a "Comments" section so people may share their own views on a breaking news item.

A simple way to offer more content is to create a user or member-generated content section. This may take the form of a bulletin board or forum, a chat section, or perhaps a way for participants to post their own mini-blogs or other relevant content. Free and open source applications abound for these types of add-ons: check your hosting provider to review what they offer in terms of installable applications.

When your site is "sticky" with engaging pieces of content, your visitors will want to click through to more sections of the site, and they'll spend more time on the sections you've highlighted. Learn from your web statistics, and offer multiple creative ways to keep your visitors' interest.

Tip 46
Data Tells the Truth: Use Your Site Reports

Your data will give you a better picture of your website than any opinion; and while any number of people may have an opinion on your page content, your data reports show the honest truth about how people use your website. Use your site reports to evaluate the success of your ongoing website strategy.

By checking site reports on a weekly, monthly, or quarterly basis, you ensure a continuous stream of data to directly inform your advertising efforts, your search engine optimization efforts, choice of keywords and page content, and your overall marketing of the website.

If people click away after 5 seconds on your site, you know to improve the site stickiness. If many people visit one main page, you know to include links to additional pages from that main page. If you have a dedicated core base of visitors, open up your channels of communication to your visitors, and find out what types of products and services they'd like to see more of, either from your company or on your website.

Have you started a campaign around a particular product or individual link? Use your website statistics to monitor the effectiveness of a campaign. You may use your stats to see specific pages that draw in the most visitors.

I encourage you to use your website reporting on a regular basis and to make changes and updates based on what you find. Refrain from building a few pages and then never touching your website again. Make your website relevant, meaningful, and timely for users, and your website statistics reports will give you an excellent reading on the pulse of information flowing through your pages.

Tip 47
For Community-building: Expanding your Reach

When your website starts to reach significant amounts of traffic, you will find even more options to increase the monetization of that traffic, above and beyond the benefits and value to your business. Some methods of making money online include ad sales, text links, paid reviews, membership fees, job postings, classified advertising, product and affiliate sales, speaker fees, and even conferences and events.

As your website becomes more of a source of information to others, you may want to consider ways to bring your online visitors even more value, without being too aggressive or pushy about selling to your community. Some samples that may work very well for you and your business include the following:

Ad sales. Google AdSense is an excellent method of displaying targeted advertising on your site. As a publisher, you may choose to display small text, image, or video ads within your page content. The AdSense "widget" automatically adds the availability and relevance of the ad to your existing page content. For example, if your site focuses on gardening and you install AdSense, you will start to see advertising for garden supply companies, seeds, starts, and equipment. With AdSense you receive a small portion of funding based upon how many visitors click on your website's ads. Other sources of ad revenue abound, from ad networks like Blogher, to Amazon affiliation, to private ad sales, where you negotiate ad placement directly with a vendor.

Text links. Text links may be an additional way to share the benefit of highly targeted traffic. For example, if your target website community has an extraordinary focus on one subject, you might want to sell text links within those pages to stores or suppliers that want to access your community. For example, a site focused on parrots might offer paid text links to bird seed companies, bird play structure suppliers, or bird breeder groups.

Reviews. Depending on your site and your readers, consider reviewing services or products for a fee. Multiple opportunities exist for movie reviews, book reviews, technology "gadget" reviews, or restaurant reviews. This depends on the quality of your traffic and your website's niche:

check SponsoredReviews.com or PayPerPost.com for more ideas.

Members-only sections. Some visitors to your site may want access to more information and are willing to pay a fee for that. Consider offering a "members-only" section with regular dues which allows a visitor to participate even more within the context of your website.

Affiliate links. Offer links through a service like Commission Junction or directly from the advertiser. You may set up your site to receive a commission on any items sold through a link from your site. The requirements and efficiency of these methods vary wildly from one type to another, and even from one website to another, so these are simply suggestions. Amazon Affiliates is an easy-to-use program where you may sell books or Amazon-listed products through a store on your website.

Teleconferences. Teleconferencing with a service like FreeConference.com may be a great way to share your knowledge via phone call with interested listeners. You may even sell or offer downloadable recordings or transcriptions of your calls.

If your site is highly targeted, you may have some good opportunities with job postings, classified advertising, and product and affiliate sales. For example, if your site targets medical transcriptionists, you might want to offer a job board where employers pay a weekly or monthly fee for the option to post their job to your particular website readers. You might offer a classifieds section where readers may post announcements in the "for sale" or "wanted" sections of your site.

If you compile your existing information into e-book or hardcopy book format, you may offer sales to the product through links like CreateSpace.com or Lulu.com.

Slideshare.net provides a way for you to deliver PowerPoint presentations in a slide format. Offering links to these items may be a helpful way to increase your knowledge base and share your original research.

Finally, you may wish to set yourself up as an expert speaker or reference within your niche industry, in which case you may use your website as a platform to share your knowledge. If this is your route, consider ways to share your expertise by speaking at local, national, or international events or serving as a source for newspaper and other media articles. With a biography and photo, a transcript of recent talks, and a list of the topics you may address, you have the opportunity to market yourself as a speaker, keynoter, or panelist at events. You might even want to invite your readers directly to your own event, which you can organize on your own or with staff, associates, or colleagues.

With so many ideas on ways to share your information and build a community, consider implementing just one idea at a time, potentially starting with a blog and comments section so you may get a feel for what other interested parties might be thinking.

Summary to Keep in Mind: Measure Your Data

When I worked as an outcomes evaluator, I learned how to measure intermediate outcomes to understand progress towards overall goals. For example, if we wanted a rise in kindergarten readiness, we would document the change in a child's ability to tell the beginning, middle, and end of a story (an early signpost of literacy). For your website, set some targeted goals for what you want to accomplish and use your hard numbers to ascertain your progress towards your goals.

You might want to target numbers of unique visitors, length of time on the site, or conversion rate to clients. Any of these will be measurable through your website statistics reports.

We recommend using your weekly reports to understand your visitors, improve their experience on your site, make your site "sticker" and give you continuous feedback on how to target your site content even more. When you get to the point where your site is generating significant traffic, you have even more options to expand its capacity as a moneymaking tool to add to your streams of business income.

Ideas for links to review include:
- http://www.google.com/analytics
- http://www.google.com/webmasters
- http://www.google.com/adsense

Other links from bloggers:
- http:// www.problogger.net
- http://www.doshdosh.com
- http://www.shoemoney.com

Chapter 7: Final Tips

- Final Thoughts on Making Your Website Work
- 48. Search Engines: Use Keywords Effectively
- 49. Site maps and Robots and Spiders, Oh My!
- 50. Serving Your Clients: the Ultimate Goal
- 51. Knowledge = Results: Publish in Print, too
- Summary to Keep in Mind: Tidy Up the Loose Ends

Final Thoughts on Making Your Website Work

As women in business, we are presently and fast becoming pillars in our community. We have many connections, often serve in leadership roles on boards or within citizenship, political, and school groups, and we're usually tapped because of our "can-do" attitude and ability to actually get things done.

I believe that your website represents you and your company, and your ability to make the most of your website is simply an indicator or reflection of your company in general. Because of this, I feel it's very important for you to understand the different parts of your website and to make sure that all the pieces fit together to help your clients (or potential clients) understand your process, solve their problem, and give them important information.

I've come across many websites that contain updated or incorrect information. Sometimes the web pages raise more questions about the business instead of providing more answers! Many small steps may improve a website: inexpensive solutions include installing better navigation, creating a "Frequently Asked Questions" page, refashioning the site with a design that's more conducive to your business process, including a calendar, or even adding simple downloadable registration forms in PDF format.

The steps listed throughout this book substantially increase your website's effectiveness. Use these final steps to add the finishing touches to your website and make sure that it actually **works** for your customers, community, and clients.

A good rule of thumb is to put information on your website that you commonly need to send out via print or on the phone. Then, keep that information up-to-date!

Tip 48
Search Engines: Use Keywords Effectively

Your keywords are the eight to ten phrases that embody your business. These keywords will show up time and time again within your print marketing materials, your company mission statement, or your organizational values chart. Use these keywords to identify your company's added value and to set your business apart from others in the field.

Your web developer or search engine optimizer will help you place your chosen list of targeted keywords into your heading files and sprinkled through your site. Generic terms like "car sales" or "real estate" or "programming" work less effectively then keywords like "Audi 2000 resale" or "Portland LEED condos Pearl District" or "Ajax with PHP/mySQL." Develop a highly defined list of keywords to help target your niche within your industry and you'll have an easier time attracting people searching for those terms.

Because of your website statistics, you may edit these keywords as you review the actual search engine terms visitors use when visiting your website. Use your keywords judiciously, consistently, and constantly: by doing so, you make it easier for regular people to find and use your site.

Checklist for web keywords:
- [ ] Create an initial list of keywords that describe your business
- [ ] Refine your list and become even more specific
- [ ] 10-12 keywords or key phrases work best
- [ ] Use these keywords throughout your existing page content
- [ ] Add these keywords to new page content
- [ ] Review website reports to modify or expand your keyword list

Tip 49
Site maps and Robots and Spiders, Oh My!

It is my belief that you will want to implement as many tools as possible to help your web visitor understand your business. Tools include items on the "front end" of what the web visitor views in a browser as well as items on the "back end" of how you manage your site.

Site maps prove to be helpful because they act as an orientation key for your visitor. If a visitor gets lost, they may review the posted site map to regain their bearings, similar to when they use a key in a road map or an index in a reference book.

On the back end, a robots file (robots.txt) helps the search engines understand which parts of your website are open for review and which are closed. For example, if you need to keep your proprietary images outside of an overall search of your site, instruct your web resource person to update the robots.txt file with that specific images folder marked as "disallowed." You may also disallow password-protected files, private files, administration files, and other internal directories.

When a search engine's "spiders" go through your site, they crawl through your navigation and linked pages to store your page content into memory: these crawls determine your search engine result pages. Crawls happen on a regular basis, depending on how frequently you update your text, so submitting an auto-generated site map will help the spider and will help your overall search listings.

Your search engine listing usually has the time and date of the most recent "crawl." Check your web address within your favorite search engine, and review this listing to get a better sense of how often your site gets checked, what information shows up, and what pages may be updated, edited, or deleted from your live site.

Tip 50
Serving Your Clients: the Ultimate Goal

In general, my best piece of advice for your website is to make sure it serves your clients and potential customers well. By making sure your site stays fresh and relevant to search engines (and by extension, to the people trying to find your services and products), you **provide high quality content in a timely fashion**.

With high quality content, your site remains lively, and your visitors gain knowledge or solutions; with timely updates, your site retains relevancy, and your visitors know that the business is thriving. When you link to other high quality sites and when other high quality sites link to you, your website increases in authority (and by extension, it rises higher in search rankings). Treat your website as a legitimate and important part of your business, and make sure that your website reflects the care and attention you put into other aspects of your business.

Find or create ways to make the website valuable and meaningful to your clients. When you start with the ultimate goal of serving your clients in mind, put yourself in their shoes, and imagine the issues they're facing. Use those feelings to innovate and create more and more ways to solve problems, make tasks easier, and deliver information; you can't go wrong with this approach.

My partner likes to mention the motto "Website = Good." Having a website is good. Make your website good. A good website is a good business investment, and an excellent website is an excellent investment in your company. Your site reflects your business. Treat it as such.

Tip 51
Knowledge = Results: Publish in Print, too

For tips on publishing your knowledge, I always recommend that businesswomen set up a blog, e-zine, or regular newsletter and participate in it regularly. Posts automatically build trust and increase your search engine listings: your archive of posts will also give you an extensive, categorized, searchable inventory with your posted information.

If you don't feel competent or capable generating content, hire writers or partner with associates to increase the quality of content in your materials.

Over the course of a year or two of website updating, you may find that you have generated a large amount of content. This content may be valuable to your website visitors, and I encourage you to compile your knowledge into print format, like a PDF document for download, an e-book for sale, or a hardcover or softcover trade book. Put your knowledge into print!

For my own websites, I've generated almost two novels' worth of published information, simply from blogging a 300-word article twice or three times within a week. I've found that the direct result of sharing your knowledge is often the opportunity to do even more work, to be called upon as a speaker, or to participate on a greater scale within your naturally defined niche. Use your website and other publications to their best advantage to highlight your specific company, to share within your sphere of influence, to establish a connection with you and your team, and to provide solutions.

Your website might become a centralized reference for you and your company, so make sure it's updated!

Summary to Keep in Mind: Tidy up the Loose Ends

When you're really good at what you do, and you love to do it, your ability to share that knowledge with others shines through: you become a true resource to others, you provide real answers to real problems, and you allow many people the opportunity to use your services and products.

By using specific keywords, making sure to take care of back-end and front-end issues like site maps, robots, and search engine crawls, and by focusing on the best way to serve your clients, you'll maximize your website effectiveness.

Use articles or posts from your website to contribute to a print version of your knowledge, which adds even more relevance and opportunity to your website.

This year, I encourage you to think of at least four new ideas that will promote your website, and roll out a basic implementation of these ideas on a quarterly basis. For example, consider offering an e-book of your most recently updated information, a teleconference series, a calendar of events, an an articles list. Next, check in with your site every three months, and add in a new section with one of these items. Your business offerings, your product lines, and your list of services will grow, and you'll have more options within your company's reach.

With evaluation, you'll see which of your ideas work well, and you'll fine-tune your model so that you share your knowledge, increase your customer base, and receive significant profits through the website.

WEBSITE = GOOD

(courtesy of 10K Webdesign)

Chapter 8: Extra Special Touches

- Finishing Touches
- One-minute Primer on HTML
- Check for Errors on Forms
- Spam Catchers: Protect Yourself
- No Phishing: Protect Your Identity
- Images, Tables, and Alternative text
- Fostering Security
- Summary to Keep in Mind: Website Evolution is Natural

Finishing Touches

Your website behaves as any other aspect of your business. You want your customers to feel understood, listened to, and responded to, so follow basic rules of common sense and courtesy when implementing your business website.

You will want to know just the very basics of HTML so you may understand how your web team assembles your pages and how they display in the browser. I've included a one-minute primer for your reference.

Out of respect to your users (who are giving you precious amounts of time to interact with you via your website), there are a few additional pieces that will help their experience while visiting your web address, including: error checking on forms, spam catchers, identifying text and tables, and fostering security on your site.

These items help your site go that "extra mile" in delivering a pleasant and agreeable experience for your website visitor. While not necessary, they do help with quality and consistency on your site: your visitors will appreciate that extra attention to detail.

One-Minute Primer on HTML

If you're promoting products and services on the web, you may just have to learn a little bit about basic HTML to succeed. I don't encourage you to become a full-fledged web developer, but you definitely benefit from understanding some basics. Here's my one-minute primer below.

ONE-MINUTE PRIMER on WEB PAGES
The web is a collection of many billions of pages of all kinds of subject matter. Every single text page is hosted somewhere and the page is some variant of a text file, with an extension like .html or .htm (or .jsp, .asp, .cfm, .php, or some other variant).

You "land" on a page using your browser. The browser renders the information encoded on the page into a format you may review.

Graphics, video, and sound are different kinds of files, but they all display (with varying levels of success) in your browser.

These are the three main html codes I want you to learn:

1) Putting a "b" or a "strong" around your text text goes here makes text **bold**.

2) Putting a "i" or an "em" (for "emphasis") around your text <i>text goes here</i> makes text *italicized*.

3) Adding an "a href" makes a link, like this: <a href=http://www.yourlink.com> link </a>.

Understand that everything within the page is just like building blocks: each item (like a word or paragraph or image) is a different block added on, with the whole thing comprised of many different blocks of text.

Here's a sample: open a new text file and type this in:

<html>
<body>
This text is bold
<i>This text is italicized</i>
*Here is a line break
*
<a href=http://www.asuccessfulwoman.com>this is a link</a>
</body>
</html>

Save the text file as mytest.html and open in a browser to see how the text renders. You now have a web page!

All websites are built on these basic building blocks. Your web developer adds additional formatting tags, images, font styles, colors, and sizes, and coding to make interactive elements of the site "fit together."

That's the END of this ONE-MINUTE PRIMER.

Check for Errors on Forms

If you have a website contact or registration form, chances are high that you will start to receive visits from "Asd Fds," "Hello Hello" and other fake entrants. A simple error-checking procedure on your form helps block these unwanted contacts.

You may specify that certain fields must be filled in before the form gets submitted to you. These might include: checking that the first name and last name are different, checking the validity of the e-mail address, or requiring a comment in the subject field. Do you require an e-mail address or phone number? Do so before the form is submitted.

You may use a "captcha" to require the user to fill in randomly generated text or a numerical code. A machine may not read these, but a human with a legitimate request will fill in this information. Check http://www.recaptcha.net for a version.

If your web visitors send in inquiries, consider logging their IP address (so you may ban repeat offenders). Error-checking scripts increase the quality of your incoming e-mails and decrease the time and effort involved with dealing with "fake" information in your database.

Spam Catchers: Protect Yourself

Spam prevalence continues to rise and, in my opinion, continues to be one of the "downers" associated with dealing with e-mail. Spam constitutes about a quarter of the e-mail I receive each day; however, I don't usually see these spam messages because of my filters. Use all the tools at your disposal to put a stop to excessive spam!

Use error checking to make sure that a real human being sends you messages through your web contact form. A numerical code, math equation, or randomly generated word helps with this human recognition.

Use any options within your e-mail system to increase the spam catching. Some ideas include:
• adjusting your spam catcher to a higher setting to send spam e-mail directly to a bulk folder or your trash bin
• using word matchers to automatically delete any message with certain keywords (I specify Viagra, Lottery, Attention Barrister)
• deleting any e-mail that looks even remotely fake
• learning how to identify legitimate e-mail
• protecting your domain name from spoofing

No Phishing: Protect Your Identity

As a savvy internet consumer, you will probably be using sites like online banking, PayPal, Amazon, eBay, or Yahoo! Part of the challenge of dealing with online systems lies within auto-generated e-mails and the way some shady characters use these official-looking e-mails to "phish" (or steal) your identity. Always go to a new browser, NEVER click on a link in an e-mail.

Many e-mails "look" and "feel" authentic, but in fact they exist solely to harvest your personal and sensitive information like e-mail addresses, usernames, and passwords, or even banking information like PINS, social security numbers, or credit card numbers.

Remember: Always open up a new browser, and type in a legitimate address: NEVER click on a link sent via e-mail.

When you receive a message from an entity purporting to be your bank with an "urgent security message," exercise caution by opening a new browser and typing in the real domain name. Don't feel like you must respond to any messages that threaten account closure or drastic action. Even the

IRS does not send messages via e-mail, but some unscrupulous phishers have sent ominous e-mail addresses to harvest social security numbers and dates of birth. Always open a new browser, and manually type in the address you need (like your bank or PayPal or Yahoo!).

NEVER click on a link sent via e-mail.

Question: When do you click on a link sent via e-mail, especially when it asks for personal or financial information?

Answer: NEVER. You open a new browser and paste the correct domain name into it.

Images, Tables and Alternative Text

Refrain from assuming that everyone viewing your site has the same browser or operating system that you do. Not everyone will see the same thing you see on the browser of your home or work computer. Additionally, some of your visitors may be viewing your pages through a screen reader (which reads out the text), on a mobile device, or on a small screen. Make sure your site is accessible.

Images on any page benefit from having "alternate text" which describes the image. By adding a small tag inside the image code, you provide a way to describe that particular image, such as "company logo." Adding alternate text to your images makes the site more readable to non-sighted users. Keeping your site text-based also means search engines can read the site more efficiently.

Your page also benefits from minimal images in the layout. If your navigation is highly graphical in nature, consider switching to text-based navigation. In WYSIWYG (What You See Is What You Get) programs, the layout, with its dependency on tables, makes the code bloated and "heavy." Strive for streamlined pages and code that's easily readable.

Fostering Security

While shopping online or transacting with your credit card, you may notice a link that begins with "https://," or you'll see a key or lock on the bottom corner of your browser. Periodically you will be asked to confirm the security certificate. As a vendor, always offer secured sections within your site, particularly when you require payments or banking information online. When you demonstrate your commitment to the security of your customers, they feel better about sharing their confidential data with you.

When offering password protection or other protections on your site, add a security notice detailing the types of measures you take. This may be as simple as posting a page on "How we protect your information," or it may be as complex as detailing the different types of safeguards you have put in place on your website. Should you track cookies, sessions, or other identifying information, create and post a notice of the information you collect. Your visitors deserve to know how you are using their personal information, so keep this notice in a visible place like the footer or a sidebar of your web pages.

As an important note, if your website compiles lists of customer information for rental or resale, I highly recommend you post that information, including your policies on opting-out and what kinds of information you sell. Customers deserve this notification so they may choose whether or not to participate with you.

Do you offer an e-commerce setup or online shopping? If so, your hosting company typically offers security certificates. Install the security certificate as an added precaution and a helpful tool for providing peace of mind for your customers, some of whom will not be willing to share financial data unless your security certificate is up-to-date and intact.

Finally, realize that some web visitors may not choose to interact with your site at all, preferring instead to contact you via phone or in-person. Give your customers options such as faxing, e-mailing, or snail mailing their order information. If you must require personal information on your website, such as a requirement to set up a user account, post very clear policies on how you intend to use required information, as well as the safeguards you have in place to protect your customers' privacy.

Strive to be as unobtrusive as possible, and don't make a habit of collecting personal data; however, if you **do** collect information, make your process as secure as possible.

If you collect information, also make sure there are safeguards on handling that information. Not everyone may be allowed access to confidential data, even on a review-only basis. You may want to cordon off certain areas of the site such as e-mail records, financial records, or personal statements so only those who you've specified with having a high enough clearance may access personal details.

As a reminder, give your customers a chance to opt-out of any database that you put them in. It is frustrating for customers to continually attempt to opt-out of communications with you: give them a chance to "cut the cord" cleanly. When you offer this type of privacy, security, and courtesy, you open the door to having a much better relationship with those customers who **do** find great interest in your company products and services.

Summary to Keep in Mind: Website Evolution is Natural

Your website will continue to evolve in tandem with your business growth. When you're just starting out in your business, a 3-page, 5-page, or 20-page product site may suit your needs, but as you add more staff, services, and individual products to your inventory, your website will continue to grow.

Your website's natural evolution will go from a static, HTML site, to one managed through a content management system or web-based forms, to one with high functionality and many different moving parts. It's up to you and your team to determine your own business goals and the ways your website supports those goals.

Use your internal business planning and company strategic plan to translate into achievable and measurable website goals. Using the tips in this chapter are merely courtesies along the way to a highly functional and highly resourceful website that you provide for your customers. Above all, use common sense when interacting with clients: when you provide effective, clearly defined, and polite web pages, your clients have an established effective, clearly defined, and polite relationship with you. Encourage that process by having your web materials match your internal company policies as much as possible!

As your company evolves and your website expands, you will see even more how the overlay of your business impacts your web pages. In the future, I hope you'll join me in chuckling with nostalgia for your earlier website attempts at archives.org, which caches copies of your website from year to year.

Conclusion

My overall goal with this book and others in the series remains to provide you with targeted resources as you build your business or organization. If you currently have a website, make your website function as a trusted member of your overall team. If you are considering building a website, develop clarity, thoughtfulness and purpose around your website functioning and design, then make your website a reality.

Your website supports marketing and communication efforts, helps with standard business processes, and may even handle billing and dues-paying issues. It works around the clock for you and can be one of your most important assets. However, just like any other valued teammate, your website requires maintenance, care, and feeding. Treat your website well and it will continue to serve you well.

Please visit me online at my own website, www.ASuccessfulWoman.com.

On this community-building site, I offer additional resources, information, and tools. I've implemented a forum section for peer-to-peer discussions and news sharing. I also screen different services, review books, try new products, and provide free articles that share much of my experiences with web development and business building. If you would like to share your own business resource for other success-oriented women, please contact me for inclusion on A Successful Woman.

To implement the tips in this book, use the following "Resource List," and contact a web professional for your project. Alternatively, check your local Business Networking International, National Association of Women Business Owners group, green-certified directory, or chamber of commerce.

>   Here's to your success!
>   Monica S. Flores

Resource List

Web Design and Development	Monica S. Flores 10K Webdesign http://www.10kwebdesign.com Web design and development for women entrepreneurs, green businesses, and progressive organizations. "My team and I look forward to supporting you in your project. We work well with those who want to utilize web functionality to support their business and organizational growth."

Web Design and Development	Melinda Choudhary Pixelloom, LLC http://www.pixelloom.com We offer one-stop shopping and consulting for web site development. We also handle hosting and domain management. "Women in business face a specific set of challenges not encountered by their male counterparts. As a women-owned business, Pixelloom understands these challenges well and helps other businesses thrive in a highly competitive climate by offering them the electronic technologies and web tools they need to stay on the cutting edge of their industries and improve their bottom line."

Web Design and Development	Nikole H. Gipps NHG Consulting http://www.nhgconsulting.com NHG Consulting was founded on the idea of continually moving forward, using technology to propel us professionally and creatively. We set out to be leaders in our industry, and have clients that want the same. We provide our clients with innovative solutions delivered in a budget-conscious and timely manner. In keeping with the collaborative spirit of social media, we have created lasting relationships with strategic partners and our clients as a way of utilizing the group's knowledge to benefit all. We deliver web, print and marketing services to small businesses that were previously only available to larger corporations. "Does web planning leave you overwhelmed and frustrated? We listen to you and give you answers you can understand. We get your project done right the first time—no exceptions!"

Web Design and Development	CJ Glynn Markatalyst http://www.markatalyst.com Markatalyst can accelerate your business with unique branding and corporate identity creation, clear messaging and positioning, innovative Web design, compelling sales tools, and powerful advertising. "The key to creating a successful business is having the right balance of elements. With the right tools, resources and support everyone can move from being a bystander to being a success. By offering exceptional design and marketing services, Markatalyst is dedicated to helping small businesses excel."

Graphic Design	Cynthia Borcena See 360 Studios http://www.see360studios.com See 360 Studios is established to help small businesses grow. We understand that small businesses, like big businesses, have to achieve their marketing, business, and ROI objectives. Here at the Studios, we offer custom solutions that meet those objectives.
Flash Design and Development	Tamar Hadar Tek 212 http://www.tek212.com TEK 212, Inc. designs and develops interactive experiences to elevate your business in today's online world. We specialize in crafting websites and Flash products meant to bring your Web presence to life, offering your company and your customers a visually memorable experience.

Flash Websites	Matt Gates The Space Foundry, Inc. http://www.spacefoundry.com Flash development and animation for web applications, site navigation, and site accents.
Branding/ Marketing Collateral	Madhavi Jagdish VISHÉ, Inc. http://www.visheinc.com Vishé is an award-winning graphic design and web development agency that specializes in creating innovative solutions for clients that deliver a consistent brand message through logo development, marketing collateral and web presence.

Flash Developer	Catherine Davenport Surviving the Pixel http://www.survivingthepixel.com I am a multi-disciplined designer drawing from graphic design, animation, and 3D to create immersive interactive experiences. That's the official description. But secretly I am also a ninja. "Never be afraid to reach for what you want or to be who you are. You don't have to be any specific type of person to succeed. You just have to believe in what you're doing. When you believe, you inspire other people, too."

Print Design	Ann Jordan UNIT Collective http://www.unitcollective.com UNIT Design Collective is a multidisciplinary design firm specializing in branding strategy and brand awareness. Comprised of designers, analysts and copywriters -- and led by talented creative directors -- UNIT is truly a one-stop shop for corporate identity, marketing collateral, product packaging and environmental design. Each of us functions as an individual unit, but together we form the collaborative UNIT that creatively challenges and redefines the status quo.
Search Engine Optimization	Rob Sanders Rob Sanders Online http://www.robsandersonline.com Search engine optimization, keyword analysis, and reporting for small businesses.

Search Engine Optimization	Preston Taylor Online-Promotion.net http://www.online-promotion.net Five-member SEO/SEM family team in business since 1995. More than marketing, we deliver thousands of customers to your website. 100% positive track record, we cannot afford for anything les than remarkable success. "From the beginning, manage your business like a multinational corporation so you will know how to manage your inevitable success."
Web Video	Kamala Appel Kea Productions DV http://www.keaproductionsdv.com KEA Productions is a digital video production company headquartered in the East Bay of the San Francisco Bay Area. We specialize in providing documentary-style video production services for small businesses throughout the Greater Bay Area as well as wildlife and animal organizations worldwide.

Interactive Large-scale Solutions	Adam Kleinberg Traction http://www.tractionco.com "We're a creative agency with a digital core. We help companies develop their brands and execute marketing strategies across traditional and emerging media. At the center of all our efforts are sophisticated online solutions."

Recommended Websites

Women in Business
http://www.womenonbusiness.com
http://www.asuccessfulwoman.com
http://www.sistersinbiz.com

News
http://www.google.com/alerts
(to set up an alert specific to your interest)

Content Management Systems
http://www.joomla.org
http://www.drupal.org

Domains and Hosting
http://www.10khosting.com
http://www.godaddy.com

Made in the USA
Lexington, KY
14 July 2012